GARSTAN

GARSTANG

The Independent Chapel / Congregational Church
c. 1777–1900

Brenda M Fox

To those who have this church and town in their hearts, I dedicate this book.

Finance of publication by Garstang United Reformed Church.
First published in 2014 on behalf of the author by
Scotforth Books (www.scotforthbooks.com)
ISBN   978-1-909817-14-2
Typesetting and design by Carnegie Book Production, Lancaster.
Printed in the UK by Short Run Press

• CONTENTS •

· ACKNOWLEDGEMENTS ·

IT IS IMPOSSIBLE to thank adequately everyone who has helped me in the research and preparation of this book. Information has been gleaned from a wide variety of sources, both primary and secondary.

I am grateful to the Lancashire and Norfolk Record Offices for permission to reproduce diagrams from documents in their collections, and also to Garstang Town Trust for allowing me to copy documents they own.

I appreciate the help and advice given to me by staff at: Lancashire Record Office; Harris Reference Library, Preston; Lancaster Reference Library; St George's Chapel, Windsor; Norfolk Record Office; Exeter Cathedral Archives; and The National Archives, Kew (formerly the Public Record Office); all of which I visited personally.

Special thanks go to the following people for information given to me that I might have had difficulty finding elsewhere: Jenny Barnes, Alan and Eileen Green, Mike Hall, John Harman, Carolyn Johnson, Elsie Knight, Peter H Le Mare, Nigel Lemon, Paul Smith, Robert Stewart, David Watson, Barbara Wilkinson, Joan Wilkinson, the late Ted Cartmell and the late Albert Clayton. Thanks also to Brian and Edna Cockram, Richard Storey and Brooke Westcott for permission to print photos of their ancestors.

I would like to thank our church secretary, Stella Clarke, for writing the Foreword and introductory verse.

Posthumous thanks go to Edward Cartmell (1842–1907) whose detailed notebooks have been invaluable, particularly when one considers he was making notes for himself and his peers, not a historian writing more than a century after his death.

Posthumous thanks also go to Maria, Duchess of Gloucester (1736–1807), second daughter of Sir Edward Walpole, who made detailed notes about the family. She wrote, 'These authentic anecdotes may be important to the future historians of this country; and to them they are dedicated.'

I would particularly like to thank my daughter, Dorothy Walmsley, for her help, advice, and good humour in correcting and editing this book.

My inestimable thanks go posthumously to my co-author, the late Mrs Jessie Cole, who was writing the more recent history of the church, but unfortunately passed away leaving her work unfinished. Jessie and I shared many happy hours of research and discussion. She advised, cajoled and encouraged me, and without her help this book would not have been written.

Wherever possible I have sought permission to copy documents, photographs, etc. and I apologise if I have unknowingly infringed copyright in the use of any of these items. Whilst every effort has been made to ensure that all facts are correct, any errors are entirely my own.

I would particularly like to thank everyone at Carnegie Publishing for their help and advice in the production of this book.

Finally, I would like to thank the Revd Barry Hutchinson for commissioning me to document the history of the Church, and Garstang United Reformed Church for financing the publication. To anyone whose name I have inadvertently omitted, I sincerely apologise.

• FOREWORD •

I am a little chapel
with unpretentious ways,
beckoning the faithful
to pray and serve always.

WALKING INTO Garstang United Reformed Church for the first time nine years ago, I was greeted warmly then, looking around, my eyes lit upon the decorated panels, the tapestries and the Biblical passage traced over the arch above the gallery. The rest, as they say, is history – I stayed.

In researching and writing this history of the church, Dr Brenda Fox not only proves to be a worthy church historian, but also a skilful writer as she weaves the discovered histories from more than two centuries ago into a lively and absorbing narrative. It is due to her enthusiasm and willingness to go the extra mile that some quite obscure details have come to light which help us to appreciate the church's involvement in major events of the time.

The church has certainly been blessed with a succession of dedicated office-bearers over the years – continuing to this day thanks to the faithfulness and devotion of its elders and unfailing support of the congregation. Furthermore, as a church currently in vacancy, we find in these pages that the Independent Chapel and Congregational Church of Garstang lived through good times and lean times, and was no stranger to prolonged interregnums.

This history gives a unique insight into the life of the church and its involvement in the local community. Any research into its life after 1900 will undoubtedly bear witness to its continued commitment and both past and present members can be proud to have shared in part of the story.

Stella Clarke
Church Secretary 2009–2014

• ABOUT THE AUTHOR •

BRENDA FOX WAS BORN at Elswick in 1940, but moved to Garstang in 1962; the town she now considers home. She attended St Michaels-on-Wyre junior school and the Park School in Preston. She then worked in the Pathology Laboratory at Victoria Hospital, Blackpool, where her specialist subject was biochemistry. After a break of a few years, during which time her three daughters, Dorothy, Alison and Heather, were born, she returned to education, studying first for a BSc degree and then a PhD in organo-physical chemistry. For the next 20 years she lectured in chemistry.

She has had a lifelong interest in local history. She is a founder member of the Friends of Lancashire Archives, an organisation which supports the work of the Lancashire Record Office; she was its newsletter editor for twelve years and vice-chairman for six.

For over 50 years she has been a member of Garstang United Reformed Church (formerly the Congregational Church) and is currently president of its Women's Guild. She is also organist at Forton United Reformed Church. Her love of history, the church and the town in which she lives have combined in this book, and she hopes the reader will enjoy reading it as much as she has enjoyed writing it.

• PLATES •

• PREFACE •

GARSTANG IS A SMALL MARKET TOWN in north-west Lancashire, situated approximately half way between Preston and Lancaster. A few books have been written about various aspects of the town's history, but to date little has been written about the history of the United Reformed Church, formerly the Congregational Church, and prior to that the Independent Chapel.

When I started writing this book little was known of the first 100 years, apart from the date on which the church was thought to be founded and the names of most ministers.

Unfortunately, there are large gaps in the church records: baptisms are missing between 1837 and 1871; burials between 1800 and 1871; and all minute books prior to 1871. Where did these records go? Were they destroyed, or are they somewhere waiting to be found? I have searched all the likely record offices, libraries and archive collections, but to no avail. What happened in those years when there was a void? It has indeed been a challenge, searching for information, often in obscure places, and putting together the disparate facts in a suitable narrative. Every effort has been made to secure reliable information and all sources are referenced. Over the years new facts have continued to be found, necessitating further amendments and reorganisation of work already written; hence it has taken many years for the completion of this book.

During my research it soon became clear that there was an overlap between the history of the church, the town and events nationally. I have attempted to cover the years *c.* 1777–1900 in a more or less chronological order. Not all events are included, nor have all people involved been mentioned by name.

The Independent Chapel was the first Nonconformist place of worship to be built in Garstang. Unlike Anglican churches that are traditionally built east to west, this chapel was built north to south. It has been altered considerably over the years, with the four walls of the main body being the only parts of the original structure still in existence.

In the records the words chapel and church seem to have been interchangeable, sometimes both appearing in the same sentence. In earlier records it was known as chapel, but as the 19th century progressed it became known more often as church. The words minister and pastor were also interchangeable. All spellings are printed as written in the original records.

Apart from the deposition of the first chapel register 1784–1837 (mainly baptisms) with the Registrar General in 1837, few other documents have been deposited. It is envisaged that on completion of the church's history its records will be deposited at the Lancashire Record Office in Preston for safe keeping.

This book is an essential read for people interested not only in the history of the Independent Chapel/Congregational Church (now the United Reformed Church), but also the history of the town. Garstang has a long rich history and, where appropriate, glimpses of its past are included in this book. Several aspects of the town's history have not, until now, appeared in print. Many facts have been mentioned only briefly but, as the work is referenced, it is hoped it will provide a starting point for other researchers.

• CHAPTER ONE •

Where do we come from?

HOW AND WHY did the Independent Chapel in Garstang (later called the United Reformed Church) come into existence? To answer this question it is necessary to start from a point several centuries ago.

England had been predominantly Roman Catholic until the time of Henry VIII. Indeed, Henry was declared *Fidei Defensor* (Defender of the Faith) in 1521 by Pope Leo X for his pamphlet accusing Martin Luther of heresy. (*Fidei Defensor* abbreviated to *Fid Def* or *F D*, together with the monarch's head, appears on our coins to this day.) It was Pope Clement VII's refusal to annul Henry's marriage to Catherine of Aragon that caused the breach with Rome.[1] The first Act of Supremacy, passed in 1534, enabled Henry to substitute himself for the Pope as the Supreme Head of the Church in England, but the English Church was still, in spirit, Roman Catholic.

With the accession of his son Edward VI in 1547 the Church, under the guidance of Archbishop Thomas Cranmer, leaned towards Protestantism and the first Book of Common Prayer appeared.

Papal authority was restored when Mary, only daughter of Henry VIII and Catherine of Aragon, acceded to the throne and this led to the martyrdom of many leading Protestants, including Cranmer who was burnt at the stake.[2]

Elizabeth I succeeded her half-sister, Mary, reigning from 1558 to 1603. She was the daughter of Henry's second wife, Anne Boleyn, who had shown sympathetic leanings towards those who wished to reform the Church. Soon after Elizabeth's accession much legislation was passed, including the second Act of

Supremacy which established her as the Supreme Governor of the Church in England, and the Act of Uniformity which ordered the use of the Prayer Book. It was Elizabeth's desire to establish a Protestant Church that would retain much Catholic ceremonial, yet which would appeal to the vast majority of English people. It was, in effect, a middle way between Catholic and Protestant extremism. Shortly afterwards the 39 Articles were published setting out the framework of belief and organisation for the future Church of England, or Anglican Church. These articles were set out in such a way that the majority of people in the country could be embraced within the Church. They did, however, exclude Roman Catholics on the one hand and extreme Protestants, who wished to purify the Church of all Catholic practices, on the other. Under Elizabeth's reign the future character of the Church of England was established as the state religion, with the reigning monarch as its Supreme Head.

During her reign a tiny minority of Christians openly questioned whether the Church should be governed by the Queen or Christ. They felt compelled to break away from the Church and formed their own 'Separatist' congregations. Henry Barrow and John Greenwood were two of the earliest advocates of Separatism. They were imprisoned in Fleet prison for almost seven years for attacking the Church of England and the ecclesiastical supremacy of the Queen. Found guilty, they were hanged at Tyburn on April 6th 1593: many scholars mark this as the beginning of the break with the established Church.[3]

Elizabeth's successor, James I of England and VI of Scotland, was determined to bring the whole country under its 'National Church'. He is said to have declared of Nonconformists, 'I will make them conform or else I will harry them out of the land.'[4] James, however, commissioned one of our greatest treasures: The King James Bible. The cause of the Nonconformists fared no better under the next monarch, James's son, Charles I.

The years of the Commonwealth and the Protectorate of Oliver Cromwell (1649–1660) brought a lull in the persecution of Nonconformists and they were free to worship in their own way without fear of reprisal.

The restoration of the monarchy and the accession of Charles II, in 1660, saw the restoration of Anglicanism. The 1st Earl of Clarendon, the king's chief advisor, was instrumental in the passing of a series of Acts, known as the Clarendon Code. These Acts penalised those who would not conform. They were punished for worshipping in buildings other than Established Churches, prevented from holding religious services within five miles of the nearest town, debarred from holding municipal office, prohibited from any position of trust in civil or military service, and had many educational opportunities denied them.[5, 6] It was many years before some of these Acts were repealed. All ministers were required to be episcopally ordained and to accept the Book of Common Prayer. Those who did not conform were ejected from their parish churches on August 24th (St Bartholomew's day) 1662. This date became known as The Great Ejection or Black Bartholomew's Day as almost 2000 ministers were ejected from their parish churches; their only crime being that they could not, in conscience, give their 'unfeigned assent and consent to everything contained in the Book of Common Prayer'.[7] Black Bartholomew's Day was a reference to the fact that it occurred on the anniversary of the Saint Bartholomew's Day massacre of 1572 when more than 70,000 Huguenots (French Protestants) were slaughtered for their Protestant beliefs.[8]

The Separatists later became known as Dissenters and Independents. The names Independent and Congregational began to be used about 1640. The former marked a religious independence of bishop, parliament or monarch. Congregational indicated a belief that each church should have Christ as its only head and should have the power to elect and ordain its own ministers.

When Nonconformity first arose in Garstang is not known. However, Isaac Ambrose, vicar of the parish church of Garstang (now St Helen's, Churchtown), 1655–1662, is known to have had Nonconformist sympathies (Plate 1.1).[9, 10, 11] Born at Ormskirk, the son of a vicar, he was a well-educated man, graduating with a BA degree from Brasenose College, Oxford, and an MA from Magdelen College, Cambridge. Some time before 1633 he was appointed to the office of King's Preacher on a stipend of £50 per annum, paid by the King. He was based at Garstang (St Helen's, Churchtown), where

his first child was baptised in 1633. The function of a King's Preacher was to convert Roman Catholics to the established Church. This office was peculiar to Lancashire, the reason being that Lancashire was slow to become Protestant after the Reformation and was reputed to be the most Catholic Shire in England. The King's Preachers were highly educated men who spoke in an eloquent and persuasive

Plate 1.1 The Reverend Isaac Ambrose of Garstang and Preston.[18]

manner. Many of the early King's Preachers had little success and had diffi-culty making themselves understood by Lancashire congregations as, not being Lancashire men, it is probable they could not understand the dialect. Ambrose, however, born to Lancashire parents would have had few prob-lems.[12] He remained at Garstang until he was appointed to the vicarage in Preston in 1640–41. He was listed among the burgesses of Preston the following year and probably took part in the Preston Guild celebrations of 1642.[13] (Burgesses were the most important and influential people in the town.) By this time Ambrose is known to have embraced Nonconformist principles and a Parliamentary survey of 1650 records that Ambrose, vicar of Preston, was a 'painful minister'.[14] Ambrose used to spend one month each year living apart from civilisation. He lived like a hermit in a small hut in Woodacre wood, not far from Garstang, where he spent time in medita-tion and prayer.[15] He was also a prolific writer. The people of Garstang had great respect for Ambrose during the years he lived and preached amongst them, being sympathetic to his beliefs and style of preaching that, when the vicarage of Garstang (St Helen's, Churchtown) became vacant in 1645, they petitioned he should become their vicar, but to no avail. They continued to petition for the next 10 years until, when Ambrose had begun to fail in health and the vicarage was once more vacant, their request was granted. Ambrose spent seven very successful years at Garstang (St Helen's, Churchtown) where he had a large following (Plate 1.2).[16]

The restoration of the monarchy and the accession of Charles II brought with it a reversion to episcopacy and the acceptance of the Book of Common Prayer. Being a Nonconformist by conviction Ambrose was a victim of the St Bartholomew's day evictions. He returned to live in Preston where friends from Garstang often visited him. During one of their visits he 'discoursed freely with them and gave them good counsel' and told them he had completed all his religious writings and had, the previous evening, sent them to be printed. He accompanied his friends to their horses, and when he returned to the house:

> ...he shut himself in his parlour, the place of his soliloquy, medita-tion and prayer. Being thought to stay long, the door was opened and he was found just expiring. This was in the year 1664. He was 59 years of age. He was holy in his life, happy in his death and honoured by God and all good men.[17]

It is possible that some descendants of his adherents were founders of the Independent Chapel, Garstang.

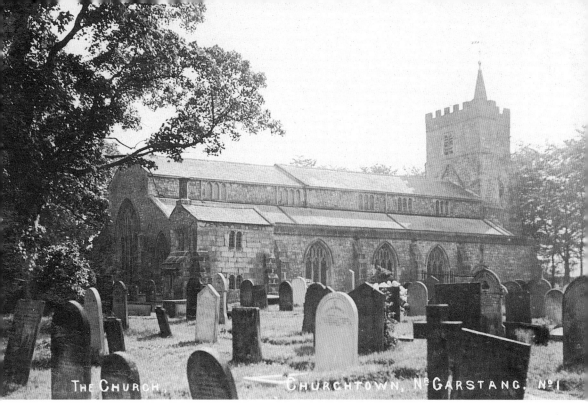

Plate 1.2 St Helen's, Churchtown (formerly Garstang Parish Church) Postcard *c.* 1906.

Two hundred and fifty years after the Great Ejection members of Garstang Congregational Church commemorated the event. The Preston Guardian, 22nd June 1912, reported:

> An instructive and inspiring gathering in commemoration of the ejection of 1662 took place on Thursday at Garstang Congregational Church at 2 o'clock in the afternoon and enjoyed a walk to Churchtown where they inspected the old parish church and the ancient register.

One hundred years later, on Monday 7th May 2012, many members and friends met at Garstang United Reformed Church to commemorate the 350th anniversary of the Great Ejection, and to re-enact the walk of 1912. At Churchtown they were taken around the old church, shown copies of the ancient register and then partook of a picnic lunch in the old school-room. The warm welcome they received at St Helen's, Churchtown (formerly Garstang parish church), was in stark contrast to the events of 350 years earlier.

• CHAPTER TWO •

The foundation of the Chapel

I T IS GENERALLY THOUGHT that the Independent Chapel in Garstang was
founded in 1777.[1] Although sources vary as to the exact date, they all agree
it was in the late 1770s. The Lancashire Congregational Calendar (1867–71)
states the chapel was erected in 1776.[2] In his book, *Lancashire Nonconformity*,
the Revd B Nightingale suggests possible dates in the late 1770s. In the diary
of the Revd George Burder of Lancaster the entry for October 19th 1777 reads,
'On [the] Lord's Day I preached at Garstang in the morning and afternoon'.[3]
The Revd Burder was, for six years, minister of High Street Chapel, Lancaster.
He was one of the founding members of the London Missionary Society
and was for several years its secretary. In 1783, when he was contemplating
moving away from Lancaster he wrote:

> My principle usefulness, I apprehend, was in being instrumental
> in introducing the gospel, or assisting in introducing it in Kendal,
> Bootle, Garstang, Preston and some other places.[4]

According to an old almanac Garstang Chapel is said to have been opened on
August 4th 1779 when a Mr Priestly and a Mr Hill were the preachers.[5]

In 1776 a Captain Jonathan Scott, who had served in the 7th Dragoons, was
ordained at Lancaster as a 'presbyter or teacher at large' by three Independent
ministers, one of whom was the Revd Abram Allot of Forton. Scott's task was
to support existing chapels and to help in the foundation of new ones. If
an area was without a chapel, then itinerant preachers would be invited to

preach in cottages, farmhouse kitchens, barns and taverns.[6] It is known Scott preached in Preston, Elswick, Ulverston, Garstang, Lancaster and the Fylde.[7] Among chapels already in existence were: Elswick (1649); Lancaster, High Street (1770); and Ulverston (1776), and he may have supported the foundation of the Chapel at Garstang.[8]

The Preston Guardian, April 18th 1868, reported that about a century

Plate 2.1 Part of Map (1756) accompanying 'Lease of Land on which to build a School'.
(X indicates site of future chapel.)

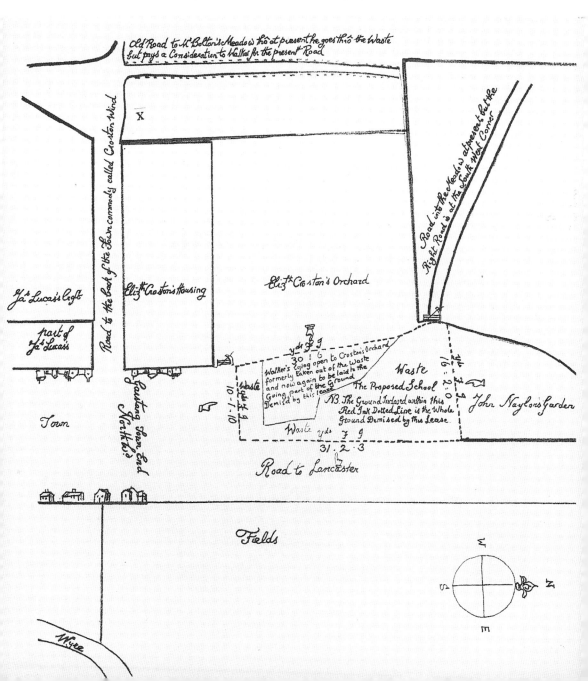

earlier the Independents of Garstang had leased a plot of land in Back Lane (now Croston Road) from the Keppel family, and on it erected a chapel. (The lease was, in fact, obtained from Sir Edward Walpole, Lord of the Manor at the time.)

A map of 1756 (Plate 2.1) shows the site on which a Grammar School was to be built, and Elizabeth Croston's housing on what is now Croston Road. Empty fields to the west of these houses mark the site where the chapel would be erected 20 years later.[9]

A religious census made by the churchwardens of Garstang (St Helen's, Churchtown), in 1755, recorded the following families living within the parish: 18 Dissenter; 154 Papist; and 461 Protestant.[10] It is likely that a group of Independents, also known as Dissenters, who had worshipped previously at either Elswick or Forton (founded 1707), felt the need for a chapel of their own.[11]

James Edmondson of Brock was possibly one of the prime movers in the foundation of the Chapel at Garstang. John Wesley counted him among his friends. The entry in Wesley's journal for Wednesday April 10th 1765 reads:

> Saturday 6th April I returned to Liverpool [intending to sail to Ireland] and on Wednesday 10th, the wind continuing west, I set

Plate 2.2 Brook House, Brock, where John Wesley stayed. (Photo *c.* 1950)

Brook House, Brock.

out northward, and in the evening found a friend's house, James Edmondson's, near Garstang.

His entry for Sunday 8th April 1770 records that once again he visited James Edmondson and whilst there preached to a few serious people.

James Edmondson and his wife, Jennet, lived in a large house at Brock, now known as Brook House (Plate 2.2). At the rear of the house, in the walls of an outhouse, are bricked up pointed windows which suggest that at one time they may have been part of a chapel.[12, 13] Edmondson was a flaxman of considerable financial means and left 'not more than £5000', according to his will, January 1793. Richard Allen, when writing *The History of Methodism in Preston*, interviewed Dr William Bell, secretary of Garstang Independent Chapel, and wrote:

> By the courtesy of Dr Bell, of Garstang, we are enabled to state that James Edmondson was a worthy and pious member of the Independent church; and that his remains are interred near the pulpit, in Garstang Independent Chapel.[14]

When the church was renovated and the floor replaced in 1984 some graves were disturbed and it is possible that one of them was that of James Edmondson.

Anthony Hewitson, in his book, *Our Country Churches and Chapels*, writes of Garstang Independent Chapel:

> Among the original supporters of Independency in the district were the Gardners of Bank Hall, Barnacre, the Parkers of Kelbrick, the Holkers of New Hall, the Standings of Sullom Side, the Bees and Tophams of Barnacre and the Rabys of Landskill in Catterall.[15]

During the Revd James Grimshaw's ministry, 1794–1828, a large proportion of the congregation consisted of farmers living in the Barnacre area.

Building in Garstang went on apace during the late 1700s. Within 20 years three different Christian denominations had each built a church, and before the century had ended the Lancaster canal, its wharf, bridges and aqueduct had been constructed (date on aqueduct: 1797). The canal was constructed when Garstang was held by Laura Keppel, eldest daughter of Sir Edward Walpole. (It is possible that instead of the Canal Company compensating her financially, she may have been given shares.) Her will, dated June 5th 1813, states she left shares in the Lancaster Canal to two of her daughters and a grand-daughter.

The first part of the present Anglican Church was built in Chapel Street in 1770, replacing an earlier chapel off the High Street. It was a chapel-of-ease to

Plate 2.3
St Thomas's
Church of
England.
(Photo c. 1908)

the parish church of Garstang (St Helen's, Churchtown). Records show that the 1770 building consisted of the present nave and porch, a small chancel and a small tower. The cost of erecting this chapel was £546 9s. 1½d. In 1848 the chapel was consecrated in the name of St Thomas the Apostle (Plate 2.3). It did not become a parish church until 1881, the Revd George Boys Stones was its first vicar.[16] Chapel Street then became known as Church Street.

The first Roman Catholic Church, built in 1788, fronted onto Back Lane (now Park Hill Road). The structure, which cost £600 to build, consisted of a chapel which could seat about 400 people, a sacristy, a priest's house and a few outbuildings (Plate 2.4).[17] In 1858 a new church was built over the river Wyre in Bonds and the old chapel became the Garstang Institute. The Institute was often rented by members of the Independent Chapel, as between 100 and 200 people usually attended their social events and this was the only

Plate 2.4 Part of Roman Catholic Chapel built 1788. (Photo *c.* 2009)

suitable building in the town. In later years the Institute became a cinema, a magistrates' court, a management and training centre, and today is a dental surgery.

Since the Independent Chapel, built about 1777, is on a much smaller scale than either of the other two churches it would have cost much less to build, but unfortunately no records concerning its construction have been found.

The first Wesleyan Methodist Chapel was not built until the early years of the next century. The chapel, built in 1814 at a cost of £670, was situated behind the Brown Cow, a hostelry on what was then Chapel Street. It was described as, 'a serious-looking, plain stone building, with several windows in its walls, and a little gateway in front of it.'[18] The cost of building suggests it was at least as big, if not bigger, than either the Anglican or Roman Catholic Churches. However, the Religious Census of 1851 shows it held far fewer people (see Chapter Five). The present chapel was built in 1878.

Nightingale describes the appearance of a typical Nonconformist meeting house:

> The style of architecture which predominated during the 18th century, and which lingered well into the 19th century, had a barn-like character, lying almost 'four square', and laid no claim to

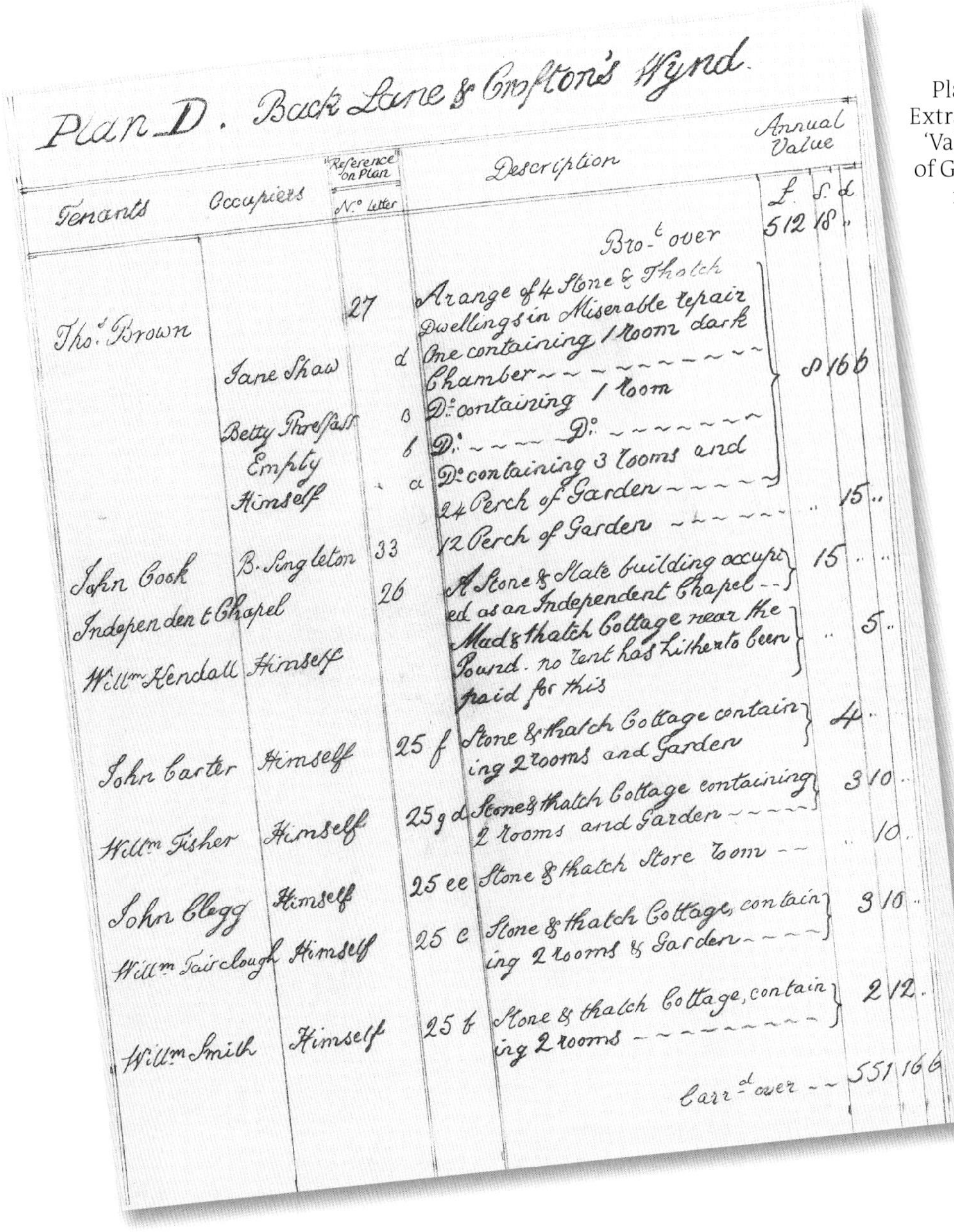

Plate 2.5
Extract from
'Valuation
of Garstang',
1840.

Plan D. Back Lane & Crofton's Wynd.

Tenants	Occupiers	Reference on Plan N.° letter	Description	Annual Value £ s. d
			Bro.ᵗ over	512 18 .
Tho.ˢ Brown		27	A range of 4 Stone & Thatch Dwellings in Miserable repair	
	Jane Shaw	d	One containing 1 room dark Chamber ~ ~ ~ ~ ~ ~	} £1 6 6
	Betty Threfall	8	D:º containing 1 room	
	Empty	8	D:. ~ ~ ~ D:º ~ ~ ~ ~	
	Himself	a	D:º containing 3 rooms and 24 Perch of Garden ~ ~ ~ ~	. 15 .
John Cook Independent Chapel	B. Singleton	33	12 Perch of Garden ~ ~ ~	15 . .
		26	A Stone & Slate building occupied as an Independent Chapel	
Will.ᵐ Kendall	Himself		Mud & thatch Cottage near the Pound. no rent has hitherto been paid for this	. 5 .
John Carter	Himself	25 f	Stone & thatch Cottage containing 2 rooms and Garden	4 .
Will.ᵐ Fisher	Himself	25 g d	Stone & thatch Cottage containing 2 rooms and Garden ~ ~ ~	3 10 .
John Clegg	Himself	25 ee	Stone & thatch Store room ~ ~	. 10 .
Will.ᵐ Fairclough	Himself	25 c	Stone & thatch Cottage, containing 2 rooms & Garden ~ ~ ~	3 10 .
Will.ᵐ Smith	Himself	25 b	Stone & thatch Cottage, containing 2 rooms ~ ~ ~ ~ ~	2 12 .
			Carr.ᵈ over ~ ~	551 16 6

architectural beauty...the interior of the church was often darkened
by heavy galleries and other obstructions...the most prominent
object was the pulpit.[19]

The Independent Chapel at Garstang fitted this description. An aisle went
down the centre of the chapel to a large communion pew where the singers
sat with their table and music stands.[20] When the chapel was first constructed,
there was no gallery. Hewitson writes:

We may observe that under the pastorate of Mr Grimshaw the chapel prospered and was the best attended place of worship in the town. Indeed the ordinary space became too small for the congregation and a gallery was erected at the expense of Mr Richard Gardner of Bank Farm, Barnacre, Mr Robert Parker of Kelbrick and Mr Samuel Raby of Landskill.[21]

The gallery went around three sides of the chapel and a pulpit of considerable height stood at the front. The chapel was illuminated by lamp light. In 1817 Thomas Shepherd was paid 5*s*. 0*d*. per annum for trimming and lighting the lamps.[22]

At the northern end of the building there is an extension built onto the original structure. No date for the ground floor addition, which doubled as both vestry and schoolroom, has been found, but it must have been prior to 1840 as in that year £38 8*s*. 9*d*. was spent on repairs to the chapel and schoolroom.[23] An upper storey was added in 1867/68.[24]

In 1984 the church underwent major renovations and repairs. During site investigations pits were dug close to the east and west walls to examine the foundations. The pit by the east wall showed three courses of stone bricks below ground level extending to a depth of 350 mm; these were bedded on a mixture of crushed ash and sand. There was no damp course. The walls were constructed of an inner wall of stone and an outer wall of ashlar (hewn stone) with a rubble-stone filling between them.[25]

A survey of Garstang in 1840 (Plate 2.5) described the Independent Chapel as a stone and slate building. Close by the chapel stood a range of cottages: one, near the pound, was built of mud and thatch, whilst four others, built of stone and thatch, were described as being in a state of miserable repair.[26] (All that remains of the pound, or pinfold, where cattle were impounded, is a traffic roundabout on which a few trees grow.) Compared with nearby properties the chapel was indeed a building of which its members could be proud.

• CHAPTER THREE •

Early days

A NGLICAN CLERGY HAD, since 1599, made returns of baptisms and burials to the Bishop, and a rough check on the population of the country was kept by adding baptisms and deducting deaths, though from a very roughly estimated base figure. It became obvious in the late 18th century that this method of studying population increase was inaccurate and the rise in the number of chapels was put forward as one of the reasons.[1] From 1780 dissenting ministers were required to keep registers of all baptisms and burials which took place at their chapels. Initially there was suspicion about the motives behind this move, but most chapels did co-operate after about 1790.

The earliest register of Garstang Independent Chapel dates from 1784.[2] At the beginning of the register it states that the first entries were made 'Before the Act of Stamp Duty took place' and, since these entries were made in retrospect, it suggests another unofficial register was kept previously (Plate 3.1). For a number of years baptisms and burials were recorded in the same register. The first recorded baptism was:

> Edward, the son of John Standing and Rebecca his wife – Baptised October 10th 1784 by the Revd Mr Allat of Forton – In the Meeting, Garstang.

This entry showed co-operation between the chapels at Garstang and Forton then, as now. The fourth entry is the baptism of James, son of Roger and Jenny Charnock. Jenny, a daughter of James Edmondson, had been baptised

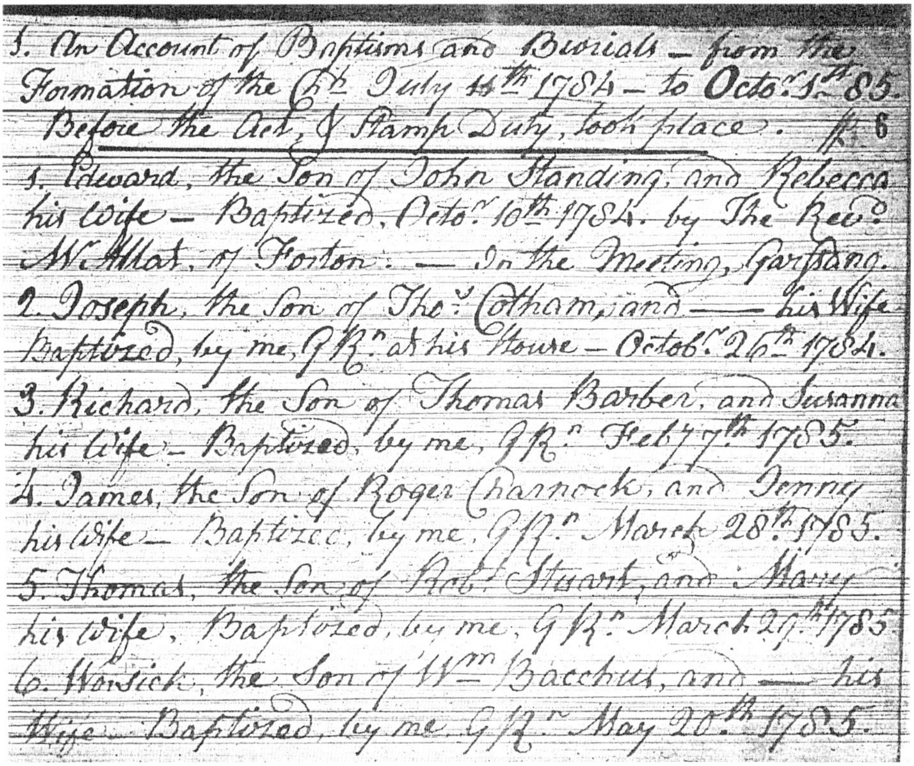

Plate 3.1 First Page of Chapel Register, 1784.

Jennet, after her mother, at Chipping in 1756.[3,4] Here the baby boy was being named after his grandfather.

George Richardson, reputed to have been the first minister of Garstang Independent Chapel, officiated on most occasions in the early part of the register and signed them with his initials G Rⁿ.

Benjamin Nightingale, writing in 1890, states:

> In the minister's house is a small library for the use of the Garstang minister in which are two books of interest. One dated 1778, is the self interpreting Bible, by John Brown of Haddington, and is thus inscribed:
>
> For the use of the minister of Garstang for the time being.
>
> Procured by Mr Robt. Gardner, Lancaster. £1 5s. 0d.
>
> Geo. Richardson, minister.
>
> The other book is Benjamin Keach's 'Key to Scripture Metaphors', dated 1779. It was procured by Mr Gardner at a cost of £1 10s. 0d.[5]

This may have been the Robert Gardner, sail-cloth manufacturer of Lancaster, who was instrumental in bringing the Revd George Burder from London to Lancaster, and who was keen to promote the Gospel in Lancaster and district.[6]

For a while after October 1785, when Stamp Duty was introduced, a tax of 3*d*. had to be paid for each baptism and burial. This proved costly for some people. John Willson, the elder, of Bilsborrow, had two children baptised on November 16th 1785 followed by the burial of one of them two days later, for which he had to pay a total of 9*d*. tax. The last date on which this tax was recorded in the register was October 26th 1787.[7]

The register shows people travelling several miles to attend chapel: from Bilsborrow, Barnacre, Nateby and Inskip (Plate 3.2), some coming from as far away as Inglewhite, Goosnargh and Pilling.

Just before Civil Registration commenced all Nonconformist registers, or copies of them, were called in by the Registrar General. In 1837, when the registers were deposited, the official name of the chapel was the 'Independent Chapel, Garstang, in the County of Lancaster'. William Bell, the chapel secretary, told the commissioners he had had custody of the registers since 1835; prior

Plate 3.2 Outlying Villages from which People Travelled.

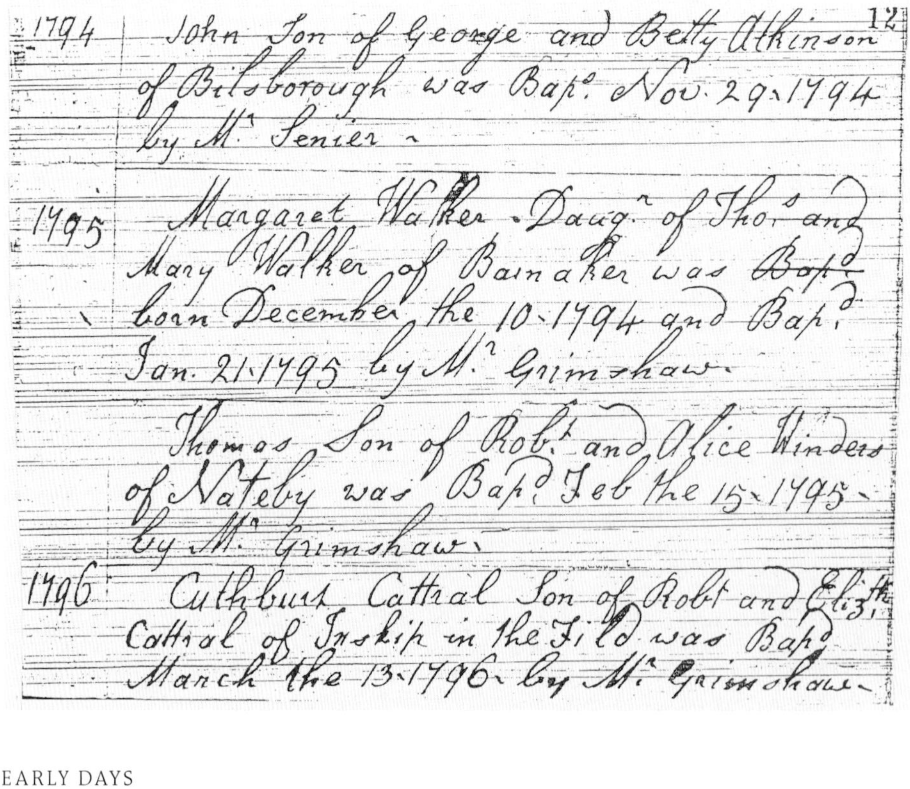

12

1794 John Son of George and Betty Atkinson
of Bilsborough was Bapd Nov. 29. 1794
by Mr Senier

1795 Margaret Walker Daugr of Thos and
Mary Walker of Barnaker was Bapd
born December the 10. 1794 and Bapd
Jan. 21. 1795 by Mr Grimshaw

Thomas Son of Robt and Alice Winders
of Nateby was Bapd Feb the 15. 1795
by Mr Grimshaw

1796 Cuthburt Cattral Son of Robt and Elizth
Cattral of Inskip in the Fild was Bapd
March the 13. 1796 by Mr Grimshaw

to that they were usually in the custody of the minister and he was depositing them in his capacity as trustee and member of the chapel. Both he and John Jowitt were the principal trustees.[8] (The Revd Edwards had left in 1835.)

Entries in the register give interesting information about people associated with the chapel. On November 10th 1833 three children were baptised: Ann, daughter of Eliza and Edward Edwards (minister); Margaret, daughter of Jannet and William Bell (surgeon and trustee); and Mary, daughter of Mary and John Jewitt, or Jowitt, (mason and trustee). The register gives no indication as to whether this was a shared ceremony, but it is possible considering the fathers' positions in the chapel.

The chapel was supported by several tradesmen. However, the majority of entries in the baptism register omit the father's occupation. Several shoemakers were mentioned, the earliest being in August 1812 when Ellen, daughter of Grace and Robert Gardner, was baptised. Other shoemakers were William Bolton of Kirkland, and Henry Kirby, John Lord and Robert Gardner (1828), all of Garstang; the latter being the husband of Nanny and may or may not have been the same Robert mentioned earlier. John Smith (tailor) and his wife Margaret, of Garstang, had seven children baptised by the Revd James Grimshaw at the same ceremony: their eldest child, Elizabeth, had been born in 1813 and their youngest, William, in 1824. Other tradesmen brought their children to be baptised. These included: Mark Standen and Mark Standing (woolcombers) of Scorton; John and Henry Sawyer (stonemasons) of Barnacre-with-Bonds; Francis Gillet (printer), John Jewitt (mason), Robert Stuart (butcher) and Henry Worswick (dyer) all of Garstang; Robert Comstive (dyer) of Catterall; and Richard Raby (farmer), of Silcock's houses, Catterall. Although the Independent Chapel advocated temperance some innkeepers brought their children for baptism. These were James and Susannah McKie (Royal Oak), and James Salthouse (Holy Lamb). The Armstrongs of the Swan Inn were also supporters of the chapel. Garstang was said to have more public houses than any other town of a similar size in the north of England.[9] In the early 1800s James Salthouse left the Holy Lamb and a Thomas Cardwell took over. A few years later a poet visiting Garstang wrote:

> *The Swan I went into and called for a dram,*
> *Then over to Cardwell's he keeps th' holy Lamb.*
> *The folk were quite civil, the liquor was strong,*
> *And one baker he sang me a comical song.*

Later in the poem:

> *Then I went to the house of one Mr McKie,*
> *He keeps "Royal Oak," you all know it, hard by.*

I walk'd into th' kitchen, as bold as a squire,
And snugly I sat myself down by the fire.[10]

The Swan Inn has been replaced by the Crown Hotel and The Holy Lamb stood just across the road. The Royal Oak still occupies a prominent position in the centre of town. Garstang Agricultural Show was held on the Chapel field (later known as the Royal Oak field) during the time the McKies were at the Royal Oak. For many years from 1818 onwards the Show Society held its annual dinner at the Royal Oak and it is recorded:

> Mr and Mrs McKie catered in the style of the times, the feast was most profuse, comprising turtle soup, game, fish, fowl, etc. and the talents of Mrs McKie as a culinary artiste received, as they deserved, the highest admiration.[11]

There was co-operation between the Nonconformist chapels in Garstang. At the baptism of Ellin Strettle on 12th April 1829 it is recorded: Mr George North the Methodist minister officiated because the Independent minister was away from home at the time.

A baptism of interest is that of William Helm, January 31st 1808. He was the son of John and Hannah Helm of Kirkland. William was, in later years, to marry Miss Margaret Frankland of Catterall and share the upbringing of her illegitimate son, Edward. The boy was to become Sir Edward Frankland, Lancashire's most famous chemist, being knighted in Queen Victoria's Diamond Jubilee Honours list of 1897. In his autobiography Edward spoke with great admiration and respect for his stepfather who had been so influential in his life.[12]

The register lists some burials, but is incomplete. The earliest grave that can be identified is that of Dr William Bell who died in 1870. Where were people buried during the previous century? Allen records that James Edmondson was buried near the pulpit; others may also have been buried within the chapel walls.[13] One family had a vault. A burial entry for June 16th 1829 reads:

> Thomas Brown the son of William and Betty Brown of Garstang was interred in the family vault which adjoins the chapel.

There is now no evidence of a vault, but it may exist beneath one of the paths adjacent to the chapel. An indenture of 1867, drawn up when land was purchased from the Keppel estate, shows an outline plan of the chapel and graveyard (Plate 3.3).[14] Land to the south and east of the chapel was being used as a graveyard. It would seem that land to the east of the chapel has been

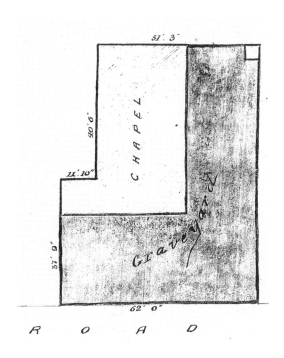

Plate 3.3. Ground-floor plan of Chapel and Graveyard from an Indenture dated 16th March 1867.

used twice. The gravestones we now see record people buried in the upper layer.

The oldest legible gravestone in the churchyard is a memorial to William Armstrong and family. William Armstrong died in 1809 aged 67 years, 32 years after the church was founded. He must have had some association with the church to have been buried in its grounds; he may have been one of its earliest members. His will records that he left 'not more than £1,500' and that he had been a husbandman of Kirkland. To his wife, Betty, he left:

> ...for her use during the term of her natural life one bed, bedsteads and suitable bed 'cloaths' and as many goods as will furnish a room.[15]

Betty (née Topham), however, predeceased him by a few months.[16] This slate headstone has weathered better than many of the sandstone ones and is now set against the boundary wall near the west wall of the church. For many years until 1984 it had stood against the porch wall facing the Sunday school. Another headstone of sandstone was also moved to the boundary wall and the name John Standen can be deciphered with difficulty. Could this man be related to the William Standen, husbandman of Claughton who, in his will dated 1851, left a bequest of five pounds, 'for the benefit and advantage of the Independent Chapel of Garstang'? When the church was renovated in 1984 no objections were raised to the relocation of these memorial stones. The exact burial sites of the people to whom they relate are unknown and their names do not appear in the register. It is possible that a separate burial register did exist, covering burials in the early 19th century but, if so, its whereabouts is unknown.

• CHAPTER FOUR •

William Bell MD (1789–1870)

A HISTORY OF THE INDEPENDENT CHAPEL would be incomplete without a tribute to one of its early stalwarts, Dr William Bell (Plate 4.1).[1,2] He supported the chapel during good times and bad and, during the 40 years he lived at Garstang, held many important positions in both church and town.

He was born in Glasgow on August 12th 1789, into a talented family. His father was a manufacturer and his father's cousin, Henry Bell, produced the first seagoing steamship in Europe, The Comet, which was built in Scotland on the Clyde.[3]

His parents were staunch Presbyterians and during his early life it was his ambition to become a minister of the Church. His first degree was that of Master of Arts from Glasgow University. However, he had a slight speech impediment which caused him to speak slowly and hesitatingly, and it is possible that this was the reason for his decision to enter the medical profession rather than the Church. He continued his studies at Glasgow University, graduating with both a Doctor of Medicine degree and a diploma of the Faculty of Physicians and Surgeons.

Whilst living in Scotland he was greatly influenced by a friend who had visited Great Eccleston, and he subsequently resolved to live there. He moved to Great Eccleston on August 16th 1819 and the following year married Miss Janet McGilchrist at Larbert Chapel, Stirlingshire.[4,5] He practiced in Great Eccleston for ten years (1819–1829) and it was whilst living there that his older children were born. The nearest Independent Chapel was at Elswick, some two miles distant, and probably his older children were baptised there. It is impossible to prove this as the baptism registers for the relevant years were destroyed in a fire.[6] In 1829 Dr Bell and family moved to Garstang where he lived for the rest of his life.

On moving to Garstang he threw himself into the work of the Independent Chapel. For some years before he moved to Garstang there were problems in the chapel. In 1792 the Revd James Grimshaw became the minister at Forton and in addition took over the pastorate at Garstang a few years later, preaching at Forton in the morning and Garstang in the afternoon and evening.[7, 8] In his later years farmers from Barnacre, who attended morning service at Forton, would transport their minister to Garstang in their carts, cushioned on a bed of hay.[9] (This was in the days before motorised transport, and when many roads were little more than potholed tracks.)

Nightingale wrote:

> Mr Grimshaw appears to have been singularly quaint both in manners and dress, wearing silk stockings and knee breeches.[10]

In February 1828, at the age of 86, the Revd Grimshaw resigned the pastorate at Garstang but continued with that at Forton until a few years before his death at the age of 96. He had had charge of the two chapels for 34 years. For some years before he resigned from Garstang he had been prevented from carrying out his duties effectively owing to a combination of old age and infirmity and, as a result, the number of worshippers at Garstang had fallen. At a meeting of the Preston district of the Congregational Union in March 1823 the following resolution was passed:

> the Revd D Edwards and E Dawson, Esq., be deputed by this meeting to wait on the Revd Mr Grimshaw, of Garstang, with a view to devise some plan to revive the interests of religion at that place.[11]

The Revd D Edwards was the minister at Elswick and, if William Bell did attend Elswick Chapel, he would have been aware of problems at Garstang before he moved there.

Plate 4.1 Dr Bell and his signature.

On January 1st 1829 the Revd Edward Edwards, a former student of Blackburn Academy, took over the pastorate of Garstang on a one year appointment.[12] It was reported that the chapel at Garstang had become 'disorganised' and it was decided that the chapel would join the Lancashire Congregational Union. At that time the chapel had only ten members, but numerous adherents. The Union gave support and guidance to its member churches as well as giving financial aid towards the preaching of the gospel. Those churches with a more than adequate income donated money to the Union to be distributed among those churches who wished to appoint a resident minister but did not have the finances to do so. The Revd Edwards must have impressed the congregation as he was given a unanimous invitation to become their full time minister following his ordination in June 1829.

All was not well, however, and even though the congregation had decreased during the last few years of the Revd Grimshaw's ministry, some still preferred his 'Calvanistic' style of preaching to that of the Revd Edwards. Disagreements arose within the chapel and the congregation started to fragment. Several people left to form a 'Particular Baptist Chapel' at Nateby, a few miles west of Garstang, and others started to worship in a farmhouse at Barnacre.[13, 14] The size of the congregation decreased owing not only to the breakaway, but also to two other separate events which rocked the local community: an extremely bad harvest in the Autumn of 1829, was followed by the collapse of Fielding's calico printworks shortly afterwards.[15, 16] In 1816 a continental traveller visiting Henry Fielding and Brothers, calico printers of nearby Catterall, reported he had been 'shown all the machines in this gigantic establishment and that Mr Fielding was the biggest calico printer in England'.[17] At its peak Fieldings employed 600 people.[18] The bad harvest and the failure of the main employer in the area combined to cause immense hardship. A meeting was called at Garstang town hall to consider the distressed state of the poor and a public subscription was opened.[19] In December 1830 Frederick Walpole Keppel, who had inherited the township of Garstang earlier that year, attempted to reduce the poverty of his tenants by returning 10% of the half year's rent paid the previous Martinmas (11 November 1830). The chapel too, as a tenant of the estate, would have received a rebate.[20] The population around Garstang dropped by several hundred within a very short space of time. The 1821 census of Catterall recorded 704 residents but by 1831 there were only 457. The report from the chapel to the Preston district of the Lancashire Congregational Union in March 1831 stated 'Many families have removed on account of the stoppage of a manufacturing establishment and the congregations have decreased.'

The following year was no better with the report from Garstang stating that the congregations were still affected by the failure of the neighbouring printworks.[21] However, over the following two years the congregations did improve and there was a big increase in the number of children attending Sunday school.[22]

The year after Dr Bell came to Garstang the chapel submitted a petition to the House of Lords to abolish slavery. Many years earlier, in 1807, the Abolition of the Slave Trade Act received Royal Assent. This Act made it illegal to carry slaves in British ships, but it did not abolish slavery itself.[23] During the 1820s people began to question the appalling treatment of those already enslaved. In 1830 a new Lord Chancellor, Lord Brougham, was appointed. He declared, 'The Abolition of Negro slavery is of paramount importance ... it is the province of a wise and just government, to fulfil the duty of justice rather than mercy.' [24, 25] His appointment gave hope and encouragement to the abolitionists. Many towns, villages and churches throughout the country submitted petitions to the House of Lords requesting the banning of slavery in all its forms. Among the petitions submitted on December 20th 1830 was one from Garstang:

> ...Also, Upon reading the Petition of the Members of a Church and Congregation of Protestant Dissenters of the Independent Denomination worshipping at Garstang, in the County of Lancaster, whose Names are thereunto subscribed:[26]

How was the original petition worded? Who were the signatories? Was Dr Bell instrumental in formulating the petition? Unfortunately we will never know as the original petitions were routinely destroyed between 1834 and 1951. All that remains are lists of petitions in the indexes to House of Lords' Journals.[27]

In 1835 the Preston district of the Congregational Union held a meeting at the Temperance Hotel in Garstang. Those representing the chapel were Wm Bell, J Jowitt, W Standing and J Beasley. The report, given by the Revd Edwards, stated that preaching took place at Garstang, Churchtown and Barnacre. The congregation had increased so much at Garstang that three services were being held each Sunday and one during the week. At Churchtown and Barnacre preaching took place every other week.[28] Later that year the Revd Edwards resigned as minister and moved to Hyde, near Manchester. After his departure the chapel was supplied for some time by students from Blackburn Academy. The following year, 1836, the congregations averaged between 50 and 60 in the morning, 60 in the afternoon and 30 in the evening. The number of children in Sunday school had decreased to 40. Prayer meetings were held twice weekly. Pew rents had brought in £21. A letter from William Bell accompanied the report which stated:

> Our religious spirit has not been destroyed, but rather invigorated by our privations and difficulties in earlier years, ... we hope the worst is past and are cheered and supported by our auspicious prospects.

Nightingale, in his book entitled *Lancashire Nonconformity* states:

> Garstang Congregationalism is greatly indebted to Dr William Bell. Year by year he appeared at the County Union meetings to look after the little church he was sent to represent.[29]

The census returns of 1841 show William Bell living at 16 Chapel Street, Garstang, together with his wife, Jenet, and their seven children: William, Agnes, Jenet, James, Eliza, Margaret and Mary. A survey of Garstang, 1840, described Dr Bell's house as being built of stone and thatch and having a parlour, study, kitchen and wash house, as well as three upper rooms and three attics. Adjoining the house was a stone and slate building containing two rooms; there was also a stable, pig cot and yard.[30] In 1867, when the Lordship of Garstang was put up for sale, Dr Bell's property was described as a 'House, with Surgery, Yard and Stabling, Garden and Coach House' (Plate 4.2).[31]

		LOT ONE	
Tenant	No. on Map	Description	Quantity (acres, roods, perches)
Septimus Smith	412	The 'Brown Cow' Public house, Yard Brewhouse and Outbuildings	0 - 0 - 17
Margaret Wearden	413 415*	Stabling and Buildings 'Shovel and Broom' Public house, Brewhouse Stabling and Outbuildings	0 - 0 - 2 0 - 1 - 21
Thomas Harrison	414	Malt house	0 - 0 - 8
William Birtwistle	416	House, Garden, Yard and Fowl house	0 - 0 - 5
Agnes Stewart	417	House, Stable and Yard	0 - 0 - 5
Dr William Bell	418 419 425	House with Surgery, Yard and Stabling " Garden and Coach House	0 - 0 - 20 0 - 1 - 2

*number misprinted on sale catalogue

Plate 4.2 Extracts from Particulars of Sale for the Lordship of Garstang, 1867.

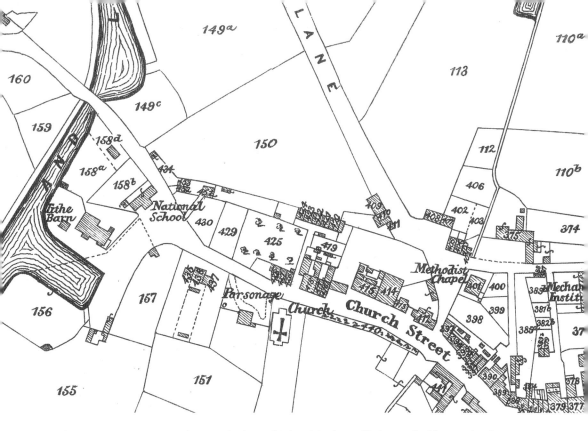

Plate 4.3 Map accompanying Particulars of Sale, 1867. (Dr Bell's house [418] opposite the Anglican Church).

Plate 4.4 House in which Dr Bell lived – left of picture (photo *c.* 2006).

The accompanying map shows it opposite the Anglican Church (Plate 4.3).[32] The house still exists (Plate 4.4). He also leased three meadows for grazing; these were called Higher Field, Lower and Middle Kettle and were off Kepple Lane, which at that time was called Kettle Lane.

He continued to educate himself about the Christian way of life and this is reflected in the magazines he read. Henry Threlfall, a Garstang ironmonger and general shopkeeper, kept a ledger recording the magazines and periodicals his customers took.[33] In 1853 Dr Bell took the Christian Penny, the Christian Witness, the Christian Treasury and the Christian Spectator. In 1859 he also took the Band of Hope Magazine (a magazine of the Temperance Society aimed at young people). A Temperance Society was started in Garstang in the early 1840s by the Revd William Craig, minister at the time.

Dr Bell was a highly respected person in both the chapel and town. In September 1864 he had the honour of Freeman of the Borough of Garstang conferred upon him. He served as a burgess of Garstang and, in 1866, was elected as bailiff of the town.[34] This was the highest office a town could confer on one of its citizens. (These were ancient offices going back many generations and were equivalent to our present mayor and town councillors.)

He was dedicated to his profession. He was a surgeon, official vaccinator and medical officer for the Garstang area for many years.[35] It had been his wish to work until the day he died, and this he did. He had been suffering from a cold for about five weeks but, apart from a few days, had continued with his duties as a doctor. On the day he died he had risen early after having been up during the night preparing medicine for a sick child and, following family prayers, he ate a hearty breakfast. He then went into the stable to harness his horse for the journey to Oakenclough, to deliver the medicine, and there he collapsed and died. He was 81 years old.

His obituary states that in his early life he had great physical vigour and endurance, and had been an excellent walker and swimmer. It goes on to describe the man's character:

> He won the respect of all who knew him. Behind a manner which to strangers sometimes appeared brusque beat a true, unsuspicious and unselfish heart. Behind the plainness of his dress and style there lay the learning of a scholar and the courtesy of a gentleman. His generous and kind consideration for others were as remarkable as the fearlessness of his character, and whilst he was never what is called 'demonstrative' his sympathy was deep, practical and abiding. He had a simplicity, a purity and strength of character which commanded confidence, and exerted a constant influence for

Plate 4.5 Dr Bell's Memorial Tablet.

IN MEMORIAM
WILLIAM BELL, M.D.
BORN AT GLASGOW 1789.
DIED AT GARSTANG 1870.

FOR FORTY YEARS HE WAS A ZEALOUS
MEMBER AND FAITHFUL OFFICE-BEARER
OF THIS CHURCH.
SKILFUL IN HIS PROFESSION, WIDE IN CULTURE,
AND FEARLESS IN POLITICS,– THE *SHINING*
VIRTUES OF HIS CHARACTER WERE HONESTY,
SIMPLICITY, AND UNSELFISHNESS, CROWNED WITH
A DEVOUT AND REVERENT SPIRIT.

"AND THUS HE BORE WITHOUT ABUSE
THE GRAND OLD NAME OF GENTLEMAN."

ERECTED 1882.

good. How frugal and plain his mode of life; how well he ordered his own household; with what cheerfulness and patience he endured the toils and trials of a country medical practice; how insatiable his love of literature, professional and general; how keen his interest in all national and political questions; with what humility, perseverance and unobtrusive zeal he laboured in the church of which he was a member; how steadfastly he adhered to his old principles as a Liberal in politics and as a Nonconformist in religion – to all these things many can testify.

As a mark of respect the members of Garstang Corporation walked at the head of the funeral procession. Following the hearse were his sons, Dr William Bell Jnr of Preston and Mr James Bell of Manchester, his brother-in-law Mr James

McGilchrist, other family members and several members of the church.[36] The Revd J Spencer, a former minister of the church, officiated at the funeral. In the eulogy he said he had known Dr Bell for many years, and had often testified to his sincerity and integrity. He was a friend to the poor, in ways and to an extent of which few were fully aware (those were the days of the workhouse). He was a sound theologian and loved to hear the great truths of the Gospel preached from the pulpit. It was in the grounds of the Independent Chapel, which he had served so faithfully during life, that he was laid to rest. A substantial gravestone marks the spot where he is buried.

A few years after his death it was decided to erect a memorial tablet to his memory in the chapel. Collections were organised and his son-in-law, the Revd Thomas Hamer, was given the responsibility of commissioning the white marble tablet which stands at the front of the church (Plate 4.5). He obtained quotes for making, inscribing and erecting the tablet; these were in the region of £20. Dr Bell's family promised to give up to £12 and the church collected £7 0s. 7d.[37]

The tablet was originally placed in the centre of the wall, above the pulpit. A short time later it was decided that the following passage of scripture should be painted on the wall around the tablet.[38]

O WORSHIP THE LORD IN THE BEAUTY OF HOLINESS

When the organ loft was built the memorial tablet was moved to the left of the pulpit and the text, which can still be seen today, was repainted around the organ loft and singing gallery.

• CHAPTER FIVE •

The mid-19th century

T HE INDEPENDENT CHAPEL was without a resident minister for almost four years following the departure of the Revd Edwards in 1835. In 1839 the Revd William Craig accepted the invitation of the chapel and became its minister. He lived in a small rented cottage in Market Place.[1, 2] Aged 44 when he moved to Garstang, he seems to have had boundless energy and enthusiasm, and was a popular minister. He came from a staunch Nonconformist family; both his father and brother were Congregational ministers.[3] When he came to Garstang the chapel had only 14 members:

> Dr and Mrs Bell, Mrs Brash and Sarah Brash, John and Mary Jowitt, Joseph Parkinson, William Standen, Elizabeth Swarbrick, Jane Parkinson, Mrs Seed, Mrs Fox, Mrs Robinson and Mrs Shrigley.

During the 7 years he ministered at Garstang a further 57 people were admitted into membership:

> Mrs Parkinson, Thomas Robinson, William Cottam, Edward and Grace Seed, James and Agnes Lofthouse, Mrs Ratcliff, Mrs Jolley, Miss Lancaster, Mr, Mrs and the Misses Irving, Mr, Mrs and the Misses Bolton, Miss Craig and Jane Craig, James McGilchrist, Daniel Stuart, Mrs Gardner, Mary Siddle, Ellin Lambert, Mr and Mrs James Parker, Joseph Chamberlane, The Misses Bell, Margaret Swarbrick, Mary Elm, John Merser, Joseph Jewell, Robert and Agnes Thornborrow, Mrs Clark, Robert, James and Mark Standing, Jane Gardner, Mr, Mrs and Hugh McKie, Mrs Raby, Mrs Preston, Mr Oxley, Benjamin Bee,

Ann Clark, Miss Park, Mary Bains, Alice Tattersal, Francis Allison, Robert Topham, George Walmsley, Thomas Rossal and Jeremiah Jowett.[4]

All these people would not have been members at the same time as during those years some would have moved away and some would have died; in 1843 there were nine funerals.[5] The list does not include people who attended chapel, but had not taken up membership.

The Revd Craig preached not only in Garstang, but also in the surrounding areas. He preached at Catterall, Caldervale, Barnacre, Winmarleigh and Pilling. The services would have been held in houses and farm buildings. In 1840 he reported that at Barnacre the average number of people meeting was 50.[6] Just over 20 years earlier Robert Parker of Barnacre had applied to the Quarter Sessions for permission to use his house and barn as a Nonconformist place of worship.[7] Unfortunately in 1841 preaching at Barnacre had to cease for want of suitable accommodation.

At that time the chapel had its own library. In 1839 a one year subscription cost 2s. 2d., but by 1852 the subscription had been reduced to 1s. 0d. for adults and 6d. for children. (This probably reflects the fact that books were being printed in greater quantities and more cheaply.) An inventory of the 257 books in the library was drawn up in November 1851. Examples of the categories and titles are:

Biographies–*Napoleon Bonaparte* and *Isaac Watts*

Religious stories–*Pilgrim's Progress* and *Paradise Lost*

Religious guides–*The Sunday School Teacher* and *A Guide for Young Disciples*

Missionary records–*In Tahiti* and *The Sandwich Islands*

History–*Annals of the Poor* and *The History of the Plague*

Travel–*Walks in London* and *Travels in Abyssinia*

Children's books–*Kindness to Animals* and *The Old Sea Captain*

Women–*The Working Man's Wife* and *The Influence of Pious Women*

The library was open to all members of the congregation and gave access to knowledge for those who perhaps had little money to buy books or who possibly had had little education.[8]

The earliest Sunday school register known to exist dates from 1838. In 1839, the year the Revd Craig arrived, there were 64 children in Sunday school divided into eight classes. The chapel was attempting to follow the ideals of Robert Raikes who founded the Sunday school movement in 1780. The Sunday school not only spread the message of faith, but for many children it was the only education they received: there was still no state elementary education system. Children were taught to read and write using religious material. Boys and girls were taught in separate classes, the youngest being put in the spelling class. As progress was made they moved up into the Testament class and, finally, into one of the Bible classes (Plate 5.1). There were nine teachers: Joseph and Robert Parkinson, John Gardner, James Ridehalgh, Jane Craig, Alice and Ann Parker, Sarah Brash and Betsy Kirby.

People could, if they wished, reserve their seat in chapel. Extracts from the Seat Rents book show that all pews were numbered and people could reserve seats by paying rent quarterly. This was standard practice in most churches during the Victorian era as it had been for centuries. Generally those who sat at the front were the main members or office bearers of the church. The price per seat and per pew depended on size and position in church.[9] Dr Bell, the church secretary, paid 10s. 0d. for a whole pew, but William Bolton paid only 6s. 0d. Benjamin Bee had two sittings in pew No.3 at 1s. 3d. each, and Margret Lancaster and Joseph Chamberlain each paid 1s. 0d. for one sitting. Those responsible for paying the pew rent were referred to as seat holders and generally had more authority in the running of the chapel than did other members. In 1840 the income for the year from seat rents was £26 15s. 10d. That same year money raised in other ways, from collections, etc., enabled £20 to be sent to the London Missionary Society and £38 8s. 9d. to be spent on repairs to the chapel and school room.[10] For most years around this time the Lancashire Congregational Union gave the chapel a grant of £30 which was to go towards the minister's stipend of £60 per year.

William Craig advocated abstinence from alcoholic liquor and founded a Temperance Society. Joseph Livesey of nearby Preston had, in 1832, founded the first Total Abstinence Society.[11] P T Winskill in his book, *The Comprehensive History of the Rise and Progress of the Temperance Reformation* writes:

> Some writers and speakers have erroneously stated that Bradford temperance hall was the first temperance hall in England, but the first building erected in this country specially for temperance purposes appears to have been at Garstang, in Lancashire, where a wooden structure was raised by voluntary labour. This building was opened on the 24th November 1834. Mr James Teare (one of Joseph Livesey's colleagues) referred to it as the Temperance Lighthouse.[12]

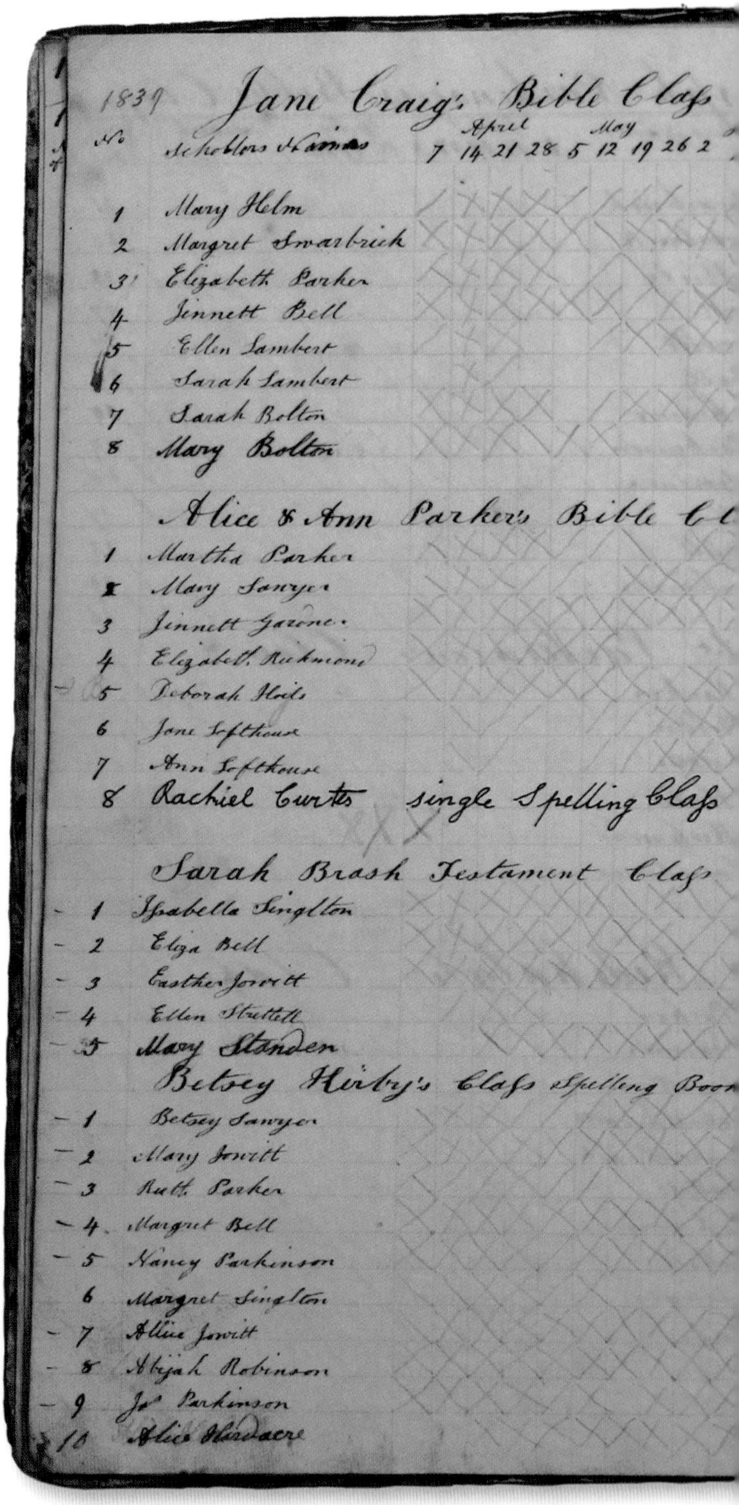

Plate 5.1
A double
page spread
from the
Sunday
School
Register,
1839 (girls
listed on the
left hand
side; boys on
the right).

1839   Jane Craig's Bible Class

No.   Scholars Names   April   May
                        7 14 21 28 5 12 19 26 2

1   Mary Helm
2   Margret Swarbrick
3   Elizabeth Parker
4   Jinnett Bell
5   Ellen Lambert
6   Sarah Lambert
7   Sarah Bolton
8   Mary Bolton

Alice & Ann Parker's Bible Cl

1   Martha Parker
2   Mary Sawyer
3   Jinnett Garone
4   Elizabeth Richmond
5   Deborah Hoile
6   Jane Lofthouse
7   Ann Lofthouse
8   Rachiel Curtis   single Spelling Class

Sarah Brash Testament Class

1   Ispabella Singlton
2   Eliza Bell
3   Easther Jowitt
4   Ellen Struttell
5   Mary Standen

Betsey Kirby's Class Spelling Book

1   Betsey Sawyer
2   Mary Jowitt
3   Ruth Parker
4   Margret Bell
5   Nancy Parkinson
6   Margret Singlton
7   Alice Jowitt
8   Abijah Robinson
9   Jo Parkinson
10   Alice Hardacre

1839 Joseph Parkinson's Bible Class

No	Schollars Names	April 7	14	21	28	May 5	12	19	26	June 2	9	16	23	30
1	Wm Swarbrick													
2	Jas Swarbrick													
3	J Jowitt													
4	Thos Kirby													
5	Jerh Jowitt													
6	Jno Parkinson													
7	Joseph Parkinson													
8	Wm Parkinson													
9	Adam Hellet													
10	Jas Bell													

Jno Gardner's Bible Class

No														
1	Edwd Gardner													
2	Jno Lofthouse													
3	Wm Stutell													
4	Thos Hoils													
5	Wm Richmond													
6	Geo Thornbarrow		Matthew Helm											
7	Wm Lord													
8	Wm Flawsher													
9	Rd Curtes		Testment											
10	Wm Heaps		Testment											

Robt Parkinsons Testament Class

No														
1	Thos Parker													
2	Thos Bolton													
3	Jno Bolton													
4	Thos Jowitt													

Jas Ridehalgh Spelling Class

No														
1	Robt Parker													
2	Robt Gardner													
3	Jno Stutell													
4	Henry Sawyer													
5	Jas Hoils													
6	Thos Brown													
7	Rd Stuttel			Rd Raby										
8	Jas Lord													
9	Thos Couperthwaite													

Representatives from the Lancashire Congregational Union held a meeting at the Temperance Hotel, Garstang, just a few months after it opened.[13] This temperance hall or hotel, seems to have had a short existence, and its whereabouts is unknown. In 1840 a survey and valuation of Garstang was carried out for Frederick Walpole Keppel (a great grandson of Sir Edward Walpole), who had inherited the town in 1830, and a temperance hall was not listed; nor was it listed on the 1841 Census.

The rules of Garstang Temperance Society were strictly adhered to by its members. Joseph Jewell had his chapel membership cancelled and was said to have been 'cut off for drunkenness'.[14]

It was with great regret that the chapel accepted the resignation of the Revd Craig in 1846, after what had been a very successful ministry.

Just over a year later the Revd John Spencer became the chapel's minister.[15] The Congregational Union gave the chapel a grant of £60 for that and the following few years to cover his stipend; this was double the grant given in previous years. After the departure of the Revd Craig there was a dramatic drop in the number of people in the congregation and children in Sunday school. In 1849 the Revd Spencer said he had been discouraged by the closure of a works at Catterall.[16] However, in February 1850, he reported:

> In a few months' time it is expected that the works at Catterall will
> be in full work and that some families may be employed who will
> attend at Garstang.

In the same report he stated that friends at Garstang had raised £33 by which the debt on the chapel had been liquidated.[17] When the chapel was renovated in 1868 Dr Bell said that it had only once been subject to alterations since it was first built. During those alterations a room, used as both vestry and Sunday school, had been built onto the northern part of the church, and it may have been because of this extension that the debt had arisen.[18]

The United Kingdom Census of 1851 recorded people residing in every household on the night of Sunday 30th March. Another census, known as the Religious Census of 1851, was conducted in the daytime of Sunday 30th March when a count was made of those attending worship at churches, chapels and meeting houses throughout the country.[19] Returns for the Independent Chapel, Garstang, provide interesting information: the chapel could seat 220 people with standing room for another 50. The following attendance figures have been taken from the census signed by the minister, John Spencer.

Sunday 30th March 1851

	Morning	Afternoon	Evening
General Congregation	65	30	8
Sunday School Scholars	35	38	—
Total	100	68	8

Another table showed the average number of attendants per Sunday during the previous twelve months.

	Morning	Afternoon	Evening
General Congregation	80	40	20
Sunday School Scholars	45	45	—
Total	125	85	20

The returns for Forton Independent Chapel are very faded, but details of the number of worshippers on Census Sunday are clearly legible and show that their congregations were about double those at Garstang.

	Morning	Afternoon	Evening
General Congregation	160	120	48
Sunday School Scholars	39	39	10
Total	199	159	58

The returns of the Independent Chapel can be compared with other places of worship in Garstang. The table below shows the total number of worshippers, including children, at each of the services on Census Sunday.

	Sittings	Standing Room	Morning	Afternoon	Evening
Independent Chapel	220	50	100	68	8
Wesleyan Chapel	204	—	74	—	38
RC Church	408	120	501	321	—
St Thomas's, C of E	600	—	490	280	—
St Helen's, C of E (Churchtown)	1,000	—	590	475	—

It is possible the Church of England encouraged its parishioners to attend worship on that particular Sunday as it would not have wanted to lose face if fewer people attended the established Church than those of other denominations. It is probable that in most churches many people did attend more than one service in order to boost numbers.

In 1851 a large gallery went around three sides of the Independent Chapel, even so with 270 people it would have been very full. The gallery was said to be large and cumbrous, and made the chapel interior dark. The pulpit was quite tall and one of the preachers of the day recalled that when preaching from the pulpit he was able to shake hands with people in the gallery.[20]

A survey of members at the Independent Chapel in 1852 listed 36 people, six of whom had moved into the area during the previous three years. However, the following year the Revd Spencer seems to have become disheartened by a fall in the number of people attending. One person, Janet Gardner, had been excluded from membership as she had 'turned Roman Catholic'.[21] At the district meeting in 1853 the Revd Spencer stated that, on account of some members moving to other areas and the death of others, he had resolved to leave Garstang. He resigned in early 1854 but continued to reside in the neighbourhood for a short time, and occasionally preached at Garstang. He later became minister at Kirkby Lonsdale and then Inglewhite.[22]

For several years afterwards the congregation continued to dwindle and at a district meeting in 1857 Dr Bell described the state of the chapel as being very low. The situation worsened and the following year Dr Bell reported that the chapel had only eleven members, seven Sunday school scholars and one teacher. He said, 'The situation at Garstang is disheartening as ground is being lost rather than gained.' As the minister of Forton Chapel had recently tendered his resignation it was proposed that arrangements should be made to unite the churches of Garstang and Forton to ensure more continuity of preaching at Garstang. A committee consisting of six people was set up to secure this union and Edward Dawson, treasurer of the Preston district of the Congregational Union, was appointed its convenor.[23] Forton Chapel had a much larger congregation and was in a better financial position than Garstang. During the 19th century Forton was seldom without a minister, whereas there were many years when Garstang could not afford to pay a minister even with help from the County Union. In 1906 a list of churches in the Preston district still receiving aid was published. This included Garstang which between 1828 and 1906 had been given grants totalling almost £1900.[24] It is not known what proposals were made by the committee or the conclusions reached, but union of the two churches did not take place. After 1858 the Lancashire Congregational Union refused the chapel at Garstang a grant for several years. The recommendation may have been that the two churches should unite, but perhaps the people at Garstang were unwilling to co-operate, hence the refusal of the grant and the non-attendance of Garstang representatives at district meetings for a number of years.[25] Garstang was then without a resident minister for over 20 years.

• CHAPTER SIX •

Renovation and restoration 1867–68

T HE INDEPENDENT CHAPEL stands on land originally leased from Sir Edward Walpole, Lord of the Manor, for a 60 year term.[1] Sir Edward, second son of Sir Robert Walpole generally regarded as Britain's first prime minister, had in 1750 purchased the Manor of Garstang from the Crown under an Act of Parliament, and through the marriage of Laura, his eldest daughter, it had passed to the Keppel family of Norfolk.[2]

In the Spring of 1867 an advertisement appeared in a London Journal stating that the Freehold Estate of the Lordship of Garstang was to be sold by auction in London the following June. It was described as 'An estate comprising 422 acres of land with the entire town of Garstang and the fishing of the River Wyre.'[3] Included in the sale were 11 hotels and inns, 80 cottages, several farms and houses with gardens, 40 shops, three blacksmith's shops, canal wharf premises, a rope walk and manufactory, a Wesleyan Chapel, several warehouses and other premises. The estate produced an annual rental of £2707 15*s*. 3*d*.[4] The Manor of Garstang had, in 1859, been inherited by the Revd William Arnold Walpole Keppel, rector of Haynford, Norfolk, whose family seat was East Lexham Hall, Norfolk.[5] He was a great grandson of Sir Edward Walpole and it was because of his need to raise money to settle on his two nieces that he decided to sell.[6]

Prior to the sale Dr William Bell was asked by chapel members to approach the agents acting for the estate, with a view to purchasing the freehold privately. A conveyance dated 26th April 1867 transferred the freehold from the Revd W A W Keppel to Dr Bell and others for £100.[7] A local newspaper reported, 'The chapel trustees and members are the first freeholders in the whole of Garstang.'[8]

On 19th June 1867 the Lordship of Garstang was put up for auction (Plate 6.1).[9] Bidding reached £78,000, but this was below the reserve price. It was then divided into lots, but again the reserve price was not met, so the estate was withdrawn from sale.[10] There was dismay amongst the inhabitants of the town the following month when rents were increased by up to 30% and new conditions imposed on tenants in an attempt to increase the rental income and make the estate more attractive to potential buyers.[11] The rent increases did not now concern the chapel trustees. Over the following years several properties were sold privately, but it was not until 1919 that another attempt was made to sell the remaining properties by auction.[12]

Prior to purchasing the freehold the congregation had resolved to renovate the chapel as it had fallen into a state of disrepair. The acquisition of the freehold gave added impetus to their efforts. A report in the Preston Guardian stated:

> The hand of time had left its deep marks on the building; it had become a sort of tumble-down affair, the roof being in such a condition that it was scarcely safe to assemble beneath it. The congregation determined upon putting the building into a proper state of repair, and Mr Tullis, of the firm of Messrs Tullis and Cooper, contractors of Preston, was consulted, and on an examination of the edifice that gentleman gave it as his opinion that it was in a dangerous condition.[13]

The members then set about the task of planning, repairing and renovating the chapel. Fund raising was given priority in the early stages as the congregation could not afford to pay a resident minister nor could it afford hundreds of pounds for repairs. They were, however, undaunted. Pamphlets requesting donations for the repair of the chapel were circulated. These were signed by William Bell and his brother-in-law, James McGilchrist, in their capacity as deacons.[14] Donations were received from friends in Garstang and neighbouring areas. Dr Bell's youngest daughter, Mary, was enthusiastic and successful in her efforts to raise money. She travelled widely in Lancashire and even ventured into Yorkshire to solicit donations from people sympathetic to the Congregational cause.

Initially the repair work was predicted to cost about £120 but, as with many schemes of this nature, their aspirations grew until eventually a full repair and refit of the chapel was carried out, costing more than double their

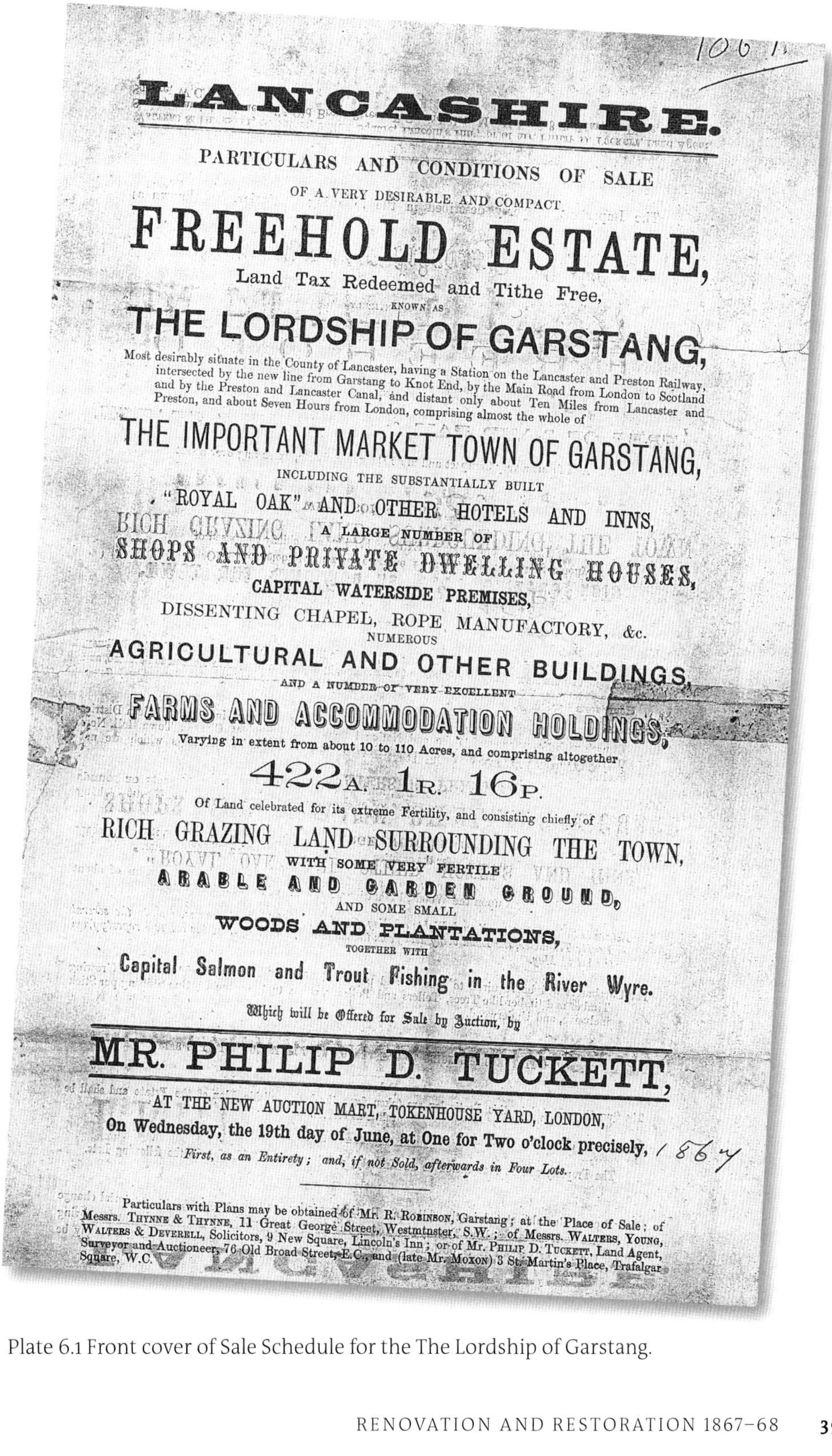

LANCASHIRE.

PARTICULARS AND CONDITIONS OF SALE

OF A VERY DESIRABLE AND COMPACT

FREEHOLD ESTATE,

Land Tax Redeemed and Tithe Free,

KNOWN AS

THE LORDSHIP OF GARSTANG,

Most desirably situate in the County of Lancaster, having a Station on the Lancaster and Preston Railway, intersected by the new line from Garstang to Knot End, by the Main Road from London to Scotland and by the Preston and Lancaster Canal, and distant only about Ten Miles from Lancaster and Preston, and about Seven Hours from London, comprising almost the whole of

THE IMPORTANT MARKET TOWN OF GARSTANG,

INCLUDING THE SUBSTANTIALLY BUILT

"ROYAL OAK" AND OTHER HOTELS AND INNS,

A LARGE NUMBER OF

SHOPS AND PRIVATE DWELLING HOUSES,

CAPITAL WATERSIDE PREMISES,

DISSENTING CHAPEL, ROPE MANUFACTORY, &c.

NUMEROUS

AGRICULTURAL AND OTHER BUILDINGS,

AND A NUMBER OF VERY EXCELLENT

FARMS AND ACCOMMODATION HOLDINGS,

Varying in extent from about 10 to 110 Acres, and comprising altogether

422A. 1R. 16P.

Of Land celebrated for its extreme Fertility, and consisting chiefly of

RICH GRAZING LAND SURROUNDING THE TOWN,

WITH SOME VERY FERTILE

ARABLE AND GARDEN GROUND,

AND SOME SMALL

WOODS AND PLANTATIONS,

TOGETHER WITH

Capital Salmon and Trout Fishing in the River Wyre.

Which will be Offered for Sale by Auction, by

MR. PHILIP D. TUCKETT,

AT THE NEW AUCTION MART, TOKENHOUSE YARD, LONDON,

On Wednesday, the 19th day of June, at One for Two o'clock precisely, 1867

First, as an Entirety; and, if not Sold, afterwards in Four Lots.

Particulars with Plans may be obtained of Mr. R. ROBINSON, Garstang; at the Place of Sale; of Messrs. THYNNE & THYNNE, 11 Great George Street, Westminster, S.W.; of Messrs. WALTERS, YOUNG, WALTERS & DEVERELL, Solicitors, 9 New Square, Lincoln's Inn; or of Mr. PHILIP D. TUCKETT, Land Agent, Surveyor and Auctioneer, 76 Old Broad Street, E.C.; and (late Mr. MOXON) 3 St. Martin's Place, Trafalgar Square, W.C.

Plate 6.1 Front cover of Sale Schedule for the The Lordship of Garstang.

original target. Estimates were obtained from contractors. The old dangerous roof was removed and the building gutted. A new roof was put in place and the antique windows replaced by larger ones of a more modern design. The huge gallery which went around three sides of the chapel, causing the interior to be dark, was removed and replaced by a smaller one constructed against the rear wall. Open benches replaced the cumbrous pews, a modern pulpit replaced the old one, the vestry was extended upwards to provide another room, and a porch was erected at the entrance. On completion of the work the interior was said to present a very light and neat appearance.[15] Further insight into the appearance of the chapel can be gained from contractors invoices.

Thomas Murgatroyd carried out most of the building work. He was responsible for plastering and whitewashing the walls, putting coping on the old vault, building the porch, pointing the outside of the chapel, and building a schoolroom over the vestry.[16] Careful inspection of the northern exterior wall shows the roof line of an earlier single storey extension with a later extension above (Plate 6.2). The window sills and lintels appear to be the originals and show a difference in style. The earlier ground floor extension has narrower sandstone sills and lintels, and these are more weathered than the upper ones.

William Alston of Glovers Court, Preston, was contracted to do most of the joinery work. Six large circular headed windows, three down each side of the building cost £1 each, unglazed. He supplied and fitted a staircase inside the chapel porch which led to the new gallery, and a second staircase which led to the new schoolroom over the vestry. He built a dais at the front of the church and supplied an oak reading desk. He also provided a cast iron stove, pipes and fittings, together with ornamental grates, and was responsible for making a closet.[17]

Jonathan Collinson of Nateby was responsible for most of the plumbing work, guttering, etc. He paid his plumbers 4s. 6d. per day. He also did some of the joinery work and painting. He painted the windows, doors, gutters, etc. as well as the front gate and numbers on the pews.[18]

The total cost of the alterations plus purchase of the freehold was £418 10s. 4½d. On completion of the building work there was a deficit of £55 18s. 3½d., much of which was offset by the £38 8s. 2d. collected at the re-opening service.[19]

During the renovations Sunday services were held in the Institute in Back Lane (formerly the Roman Catholic Chapel). Mary Bell assisted her ageing father by taking on the responsibility of organising the reopening service. At the close of the service in the chapel the congregation assembled in the Institute where, together with a large number of friends, they sat down to a substantial tea, probably feeling satisfied with what they had achieved.[20]

• CHAPTER SEVEN •

The early 1870s

C HANGES HAD TO BE MADE! The Congregational Chapel had been without a minister for 17 years and the death of Dr Bell had left a vacuum. He had been the chief decision maker in chapel affairs. Due to the intransigence of the members of Garstang Chapel to form a joint pastorate with Forton, many years earlier, the chapel had been more of a sleeping, rather than active member of the Congregational Union. Robert Mansergh, representing the Preston district of the Congregational Union, called a meeting of the chapel trustees in 1871, a few months after the death of Dr Bell. At that meeting it was decided that chapel business would, in future, be overseen by a committee, rather than a single person.

Edward Cartmell of Garstang was elected secretary and John Balderstone of Barnacre, treasurer. Other committee members were: James Clark of Pilling; Thomas Clark and Robert Singleton of Kirkland; Thomas Smith, Jonathan Jowitt Thomas and Robert Gardner of Garstang; John Cartmell of Bonds; and George Helm of Barnacre.[1] These were the forerunners of the Elders of the United Reformed Church today.

Soon afterwards a letter was received from Edward B Dawson, secretary of the Preston district, stating that the Congregational Union had made a grant of £10 to the chapel at Garstang, and he advised the chapel to become a more active member of the Union.[2] Edward Cartmell and John Balderstone were appointed delegates to the Union and, when they attended the next meeting of the Preston district, they reported:

> The ministers and delegates expressed a kind Christian feeling
> towards the Church at Garstang and unanimously voted a grant of
> £15 towards the support of the ministry.[3]

Garstang was, in effect, being welcomed back into the Congregational Union after being on the periphery for many years.

It was resolved that the chapel be registered for the solemnisation of marriages. Hardwicke's Marriage Act of 1753 had decreed that only marriages in the Anglican Church were legal and valid, although Quakers and Jews became exempt from the Act and Roman Catholics usually ignored it. Nonconformists, however, were often forced to marry in their local parish church and it was not until 1836 that this restriction was removed.[4] It is not known why Garstang did not register for marriages until 1871. Forton Chapel had registered several years previously; Dr Bell's daughter, Margaret, was married there in June 1860, to Edwin Cox, a dentist from Preston.[5]

In September 1871 Mrs Bell and family moved away from Garstang and a farewell tea was held to mark the occasion. Mary Bell, in recognition of her tireless work for the chapel, was presented with a writing case, blotter and walnut work table engraved:

> Presented by the congregation of the Independent Chapel to Miss
> Mary Bell on the occasion of her leaving Garstang as a small token
> of esteem for her incessant labours in connection with the above
> cause. Garstang September 1st 1871.[6]

Five days later Mary married the Revd Thomas Hamer, of Manchester (Plate 7.1).[7] It was appropriate that the first marriage to take place in the chapel was between two people who had served it well. Thomas Hamer had been brought up in nearby Scorton and his parents were members of Garstang Independent Chapel.[8] In the long interregnum he often preached at Garstang and chaired meetings. The following month a second marriage took place. This was between Sarah Jane Cartmell, sister of Edward Cartmell the church secretary, and William Robinson of Preston.[9]

During the long interregnum several ministers and lay preachers took services at the chapel. These included: the Revd John Spencer, a former minister; the Revd W Hudson, minister at Forton; Mr Edwin Cox of Preston; the Revd Thomas Hamer; and the Revd Ebenezer Le Mare.[10] Edwin Cox and Thomas Hamer were sons-in-law of Dr William Bell. Ebenezer Le Mare was the brother-in-law of Thomas Hamer having married Thomas's sister, Sarah Jane (Sallie) Hamer. Visiting preachers, who were ministers, were paid 10s. 0d., and lay preachers 7s. 0d.; this was for two or sometimes three

Plate 7.1 Revd Thomas Hamer and Miss Mary Bell. Photographs undated.

services on a Sunday. Some of the preachers had quite a distance to travel, so Thomas Hamer's mother provided hospitality of dinner, tea and lodgings when required. The chapel paid her 5s. 0d. for two nights' lodgings and meals for a full day, and 3s. 0d. if only dinner and tea were required.[11]

The chapel was often short of money, so the trustees decided pew rents should be abolished and a weekly offertory taken instead. Initially this was successful. In December 1871 it was reported that the offertory for the previous quarter had brought in more than pew rents would have done. However, within four years they had to revert back to pew rents as the increase in weekly offerings had not continued. In an attempt to raise chapel income it was decided that both weekly offerings be taken and pew rents paid.[12]

Mr G Green, who played the harmonium, was paid a gratuity of 10s. 0d. per annum and the harmonium was tuned annually by a Mr Hays at a cost of 5s. 0d.[13, 14]

In 1872 Anthony Hewitson visited both the town of Garstang and the Congregational Chapel. He described the town as:

...a most irregular, ricketty, tumbledown and antiquated town...The streets are paved but unless you wear shoe soles two inches thick it is torture to walk down them, and as to the lighting, why it is ante-deluvian...The inhabitants are frugal, long-lived and primitive in their habits.[15]

Of the chapel, which had fields adjacent to its north and west boundaries, he said:

It is about the size of a couple of cottages and is quite plain in its general architecture. The inside looks neat and cheerful, and is in very good order. The building will hold about 300 persons, and is attended by about 50. There were 22 present when we visited the chapel. The preacher was a clean-looking, precise-speaking, Lancaster person. The service and sermon appeared to be good; but we enjoyed neither particularly, for during the whole time a bull, or a very uneasy cow, in a field close to the chapel, kept roaring out, as if trying to get up a little opposition on its own particular account.

By 1872 the graveyard was almost full, so an approach was made to Mr Thynne, agent for the Keppel estate, with regard to purchasing a piece of land to extend the graveyard. Land from the field at the rear was offered at 5s. 0d. per square yard.[16] The committee considered this overpriced, offered half, i.e. 2s. 6d. per square yard, and this was accepted. The area of land purchased was 268 square yards. Jonathan Jowitt Thomas was appointed chairman of the new burial ground committee with William Raby of Bonds Fold and John Preston of Kiln Trees, Cabus, as committee members.[17] Pamphlets requesting donations for the extension were circulated and subscriptions collected. The committee was confident the money would be raised in just a few weeks, and it was. The price of a burial plot in the new ground was £1. Some people purchased theirs 'in advance'. Purchase of the land, lime, carting of materials and Henry Sawyer's account for building a wall to enclose the land came to £66 2s. 3d.[18] The old burial ground was declared closed in April 1874 after the burial of Samuel Strettle, aged 85 years. The only burials in the old ground after this were those in graves already in existence. John Hamer, the chapel-keeper, Thomas Hamer's father, was given the task of levelling the new burial ground and forming a walkway around the chapel.[19] In 1876 his salary was raised from £2 to £3 per annum. A few years later Thomas Grayston, who also helped look after the graveyard, landscaped the area with trees and shrubs.[20]

• CHAPTER EIGHT •

The mid to late 1870s

F OR TWENTY YEARS the Congregational Chapel had drifted along without a minister, owing mainly to a shortage of money. The deacons had worked hard to hold the congregation together but, eventually, in March 1875, they decided to advertise the vacancy and, hopefully, bring to an end the long interregnum.[1] In September of that year the Revd John Schofield was invited to become their minister. The minutes record:

> After having heard the Rev J Schofield preach on different occasions, and being highly recommended by several friends, this committee begs to offer him a most hearty and cordial invitation to accept the pastoral charge of the church and congregation assembling at the Independent Chapel Garstang. After a careful consideration of the financial condition the committee feel that they would not be justified in offering a larger salary than can be provided without incurring the risk of going into debt. They can therefore only offer him at present the sum of £52 per annum.

This resolution was submitted to the congregation on Sunday 5th of September 1875 when it was fully approved.[2]

On October 31st 1875 the Revd Schofield formally accepted the chapel's invitation. He had not come through the usual channels into the ministry. He had previously taught in a large boarding school and had been the proprietor of a private school. He also had business interests. For many years he had been a lay preacher and during that time had resolved to enter the full time ministry.[3] He was probably of short stature as the church minutes record the reading desk had to be lowered to suit his height.[4]

To welcome the Revd Schofield and to mark the end of a long interregnum it was decided to hold a celebration tea, followed by a meeting in chapel (Plate 8.1). Tea meetings were a feature of the chapel when a celebration was called for. A ladies committee was set up to organise the event. Mr Smith, treasurer, and Mr E Cartmell, secretary, assisted with ticket sales, booking of the Institute, etc. The Garstang Institute, formerly the Roman Catholic Chapel, was the only place in Garstang capable of holding the large number of people expected to attend. Tickets cost 1s. 0d. with children half price.

Several ladies promised to provide a tray of food worth either 2s. 6d., 5s. 0d. or 10s. 0d., or to give the equivalent in money. Surnames of those promising trays of food were: Thomas, Clark, Schofield, Cartmell, Rooking, Hamer, James, Smith, Robinson, Gillan, Walker, Preston, Singleton, Thompson, Jackson, Helm and Armstrong.

Plate 8.1 Tea Meeting to Welcome the Reverend John Schofield.

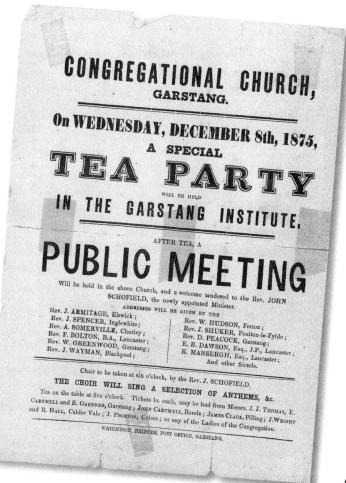

CONGREGATIONAL CHURCH, GARSTANG.

On WEDNESDAY, DECEMBER 8th, 1875, A SPECIAL

TEA PARTY

WILL BE HELD

IN THE GARSTANG INSTITUTE.

AFTER TEA, A

PUBLIC MEETING

Will be held in the above Church, and a welcome tendered to the Rev. JOHN SCHOFIELD, the newly appointed Minister.

ADDRESSES WILL BE GIVEN BY THE

Rev. J. ARMITAGE, Elswick;
Rev. J. SPENCER, Inglewhite;
Rev. A. SOMERVILLE, Chorley;
Rev. F. BOLTON, B.A., Lancaster;
Rev. W. GREENWOOD, Garstang;
Rev. J. WAYMAN, Blackpool;

Rev. W. HUDSON, Forton;
Rev. J. SHUKER, Poulton-le-Fylde;
Rev. D. PEACOCK, Garstang;
E. B. DAWSON, Esq., J.P., Lancaster;
R. MANSERGH, Esq., Lancaster;
And other friends.

Chair to be taken at six o'clock, by the Rev. J. SCHOFIELD.
THE CHOIR WILL SING A SELECTION OF ANTHEMS, &c.
Tea on the table at five o'clock. Tickets 1s. each, may be had from Messrs. J. J. THOMAS, E. CARTMELL and R. GARDNER, Garstang; JOHN CARTMELL, Bonds; JAMES CLARK, Pilling; J. WRIGHT and R. HALL, Calder Vale; J. PRESTON, Cabus; or any of the Ladies of the Congregation.

WRIGHTSON, PRINTER, POST OFFICE, GARSTANG.

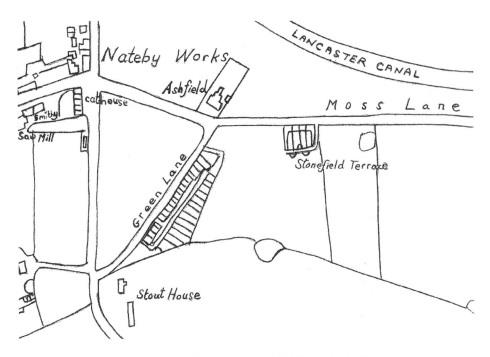

Plate 8.2 Location of the Manse, 'Ashfield', Nateby, built 1876.
Copied from Lancashire Sheet XLIV 7. Published at the Ordnance Survey Office,
Southampton, 1893.

The tea consisted of beef which cost £1 0s. 6d., weighed between 25 and 30 lbs and was cooked by Mrs Thomas, Miss Smith and Mrs E Cartmell; 15 lbs ham at 11½d. per lb; 24 lbs currant bread at 8d. per lb; 2 lbs tea at 3s. 8d. per lb; 10s. worth of plain bread; 6 lbs biscuits; 10 lbs lump sugar; 9 lbs butter; milk; cream; tartlets; and jam.

The Institute charged 2s. 6d. for the hire of their premises, 6s. 0d. for lighting and use of the tea urn, 4s. 4d. for use of crockery, etc., 7s. 11½d. for setting out the room with tables and chairs, and 10s. 0d. for heating. Other costs included visiting ministers' travelling expenses, printing, postage, etc. A total of 176 people attended the event. When all income and expenditure had been accounted for there was a small profit of £3 10s. 9d.[5]

After tea a meeting was held in the chapel when a warm welcome was extended to the new minister. The Revd J Spencer, a former minister, welcomed the Revd Schofield on behalf of the congregation. The Revd Schofield then addressed the meeting and said he was pleased to accept the chapel's invitation, and hoped he would live long amongst them and never regret the step he had taken, to which there were cheers of 'Hear, Hear!' Other speakers followed and the choir sang a selection of songs, conducted by Mr Rooking and accompanied by Mr Green on the harmonium.[6]

Plate 8.3 Ashfield, Nateby. The House on the left was the Manse. (Photo 2014)

In February 1876 the question of building a manse was raised, as the Revd Schofield and his wife were living in rented accommodation.[7] Various land-owners were approached with a view to acquiring a suitable plot. In April 1876, it was resolved that the offer of land at Nateby, as a gift from Mr Bashall Esq., be accepted with very many thanks.[8] The plot of land was on Moss Lane, almost opposite Green Lane (also called Diamond Row) (Plate 8.2). It was decided that two semi-detached houses should be built, one for the use of the minister and one to let, subject to Mr Bashall's approval. It was estimated that the houses would cost in the region of £600 to build; in fact, the final cost was over £700.[9] Each house had an attic and a servant's bedroom. A well was sunk to supply the houses with water. Members of the building committee were Revd John Schofield (chairman), Jonathan Jowitt Thomas (vice-chairman), James Clark (treasurer) and Edward Cartmell (secretary). A subscription book was opened and within a short time the money had been raised. Richard Helm of Leyland was a generous benefactor, donating £200 on condition that the trustees would agree to pay him the sum of £9 per annum to the end of his life and then to the end of that of his wife, Mrs Jane Helm, should he predecease her.[10] The houses were named 'Ashfield' (Plate 8.3).[11] In June 1876 a list of people to act as trustees of the houses was drawn up.[12]

James Clark	Farmer	Pilling
Thomas Smith	(Insurance Agent)[13]	Garstang
Robert Gardner	Shoemaker	Garstang
E Cartmell	Tailor & Draper	Garstang
John Balderstone	Farmer	Little Singleton
*E B Dawson Esq	(Barrister)[14]	Lune Cliffe, Lancaster
*Robert Mansergh	Draper, etc.	Lancaster
J J Thomas	Chemist, etc.	Garstang
John Cartmell Jnr	Tailor	Garstang
John Preston	Farmer	Cabus
Thomas Clark	Farmer	Kirkland

*E B Dawson Esq. was treasurer of the Preston district of the Lancashire Congregational Union and Robert Mansergh its secretary.

Mrs W H Storey of Halton, near Lancaster, was the first tenant of the house adjoining the manse. She agreed to take the house on a yearly rental of 19 guineas, on condition the trustees erected a laundry for her use, to which she agreed to pay an extra 19s. 0d. per annum.[15] Over the next 40 years one house continued to be let and the other was sometimes used as a manse and sometimes let. At a committee meeting in 1916 the question of whether to sell the manse and adjoining house was discussed. In 1918 when the Revd W S Rowland, the minister from Elswick, was given the pastoral oversight of the church there was no need for a manse and the two houses were sold to the Misses Willacy.[16, 17]

Following a proposal by Edward Cartmell, in January 1877, it was decided to increase the Revd Schofield's stipend to £100 per annum. Also, his stipend for the previous year was to be made up to £100 in retrospect. This followed the recommendation made by the Preston district of the Congregational Union several years previously regarding ministers' stipends.[18, 19] The Revd Schofield's stipend was to be made up of a grant of £40 from the Lancashire Congregational Union, £10 from Lady Hewley's Trust which gave grants to 'poor places of worship', £20 annual rent for the manse plus £30 to be found by the congregation.[20]

In May 1879 it was proposed that the chapel be re-decorated as soon as possible. The secretary was asked to procure tenders for the work. The doors, windows and base of the walls were to be painted, the rest of the walls colour washed and the pews varnished. It was also proposed that the square pews at the front of the church be altered and made suitable for the choir.

At a subsequent meeting it was agreed to ask Henry Waterhouse of Ivy Cottage, Garstang, to submit a tender. However, the treasurer and secretary were told to 'give the job to the person who would do it for the least money'.[21, 22]

The chapel and Sunday school anniversary was celebrated each year in June. This was an important occasion with three services on the Sunday and one on the Monday evening. Usually an eminent preacher was invited to officiate at the services. The preacher on the Monday evening of the 11th June 1877 was the Revd S Pearson, MA, of Liverpool and it was reported:

> The Revd gentleman's discourse occupied upwards of one hour in delivery, during which time he was most attentively listened to by a tolerably large congregation.[23]

In the eighteenth and nineteenth centuries it was usual to have sermons lasting over an hour. The sermon preached at Robert Dawson's funeral, held at Forton Independent Chapel, in 1769, was 23 pages long; the original can be seen at the Lancashire Record Office.[24]

The Revd Pearson was invited to the anniversary celebrations in 1879, two years after his previous visit. The chapel decided to dispense with a service on the Monday evening and instead invited him to deliver a lecture on a subject of his choice. He chose, 'The life and times of Richard Baxter' (Plate 8.4). Richard Baxter was a puritan cleric who allied himself with no particular denomination. He was a contemporary of Isaac Ambrose (Chapter 1).[25] No one seems to have given the Revd Pearson any indication of how long the lecture should last. A local newspaper reported, 'his lecture was a very lengthy one, but nevertheless listened to with marked attention.'[26]

For many years the Sunday school scholars had been given an annual treat. Usually between 40 and 50 children went on the treat, accompanied by about 40 adults, possibly their mothers. They usually travelled by horse-drawn wagonettes to their destination. In September 1876 the children were given an extra special treat – a train ride from Garstang to Pilling, followed by a meal consisting of beef, bread and butter, biscuits, buns, nuts, coffee, milk and ginger beer. For many children this would have been a great adventure. In 1877 there was a picnic at Nicky Nook, a local beauty spot, and in 1878 they picnicked at Batty's Hill, Cockerham.[27, 28]

In the 1880s and 1890s they ventured further afield, visiting Southport, Morecambe and Strawberry Gardens, Heysham. A visit to Knott End in 1895 was very popular. Edward Cartmell, church secretary, hired several wagonettes from Richard Birchall (Kenlis Arms, Barnacre), James Lees (Golden Ball Inn) and Nicholas Isles (Royal Oak Hotel).[29] The Golden Ball Inn was at the

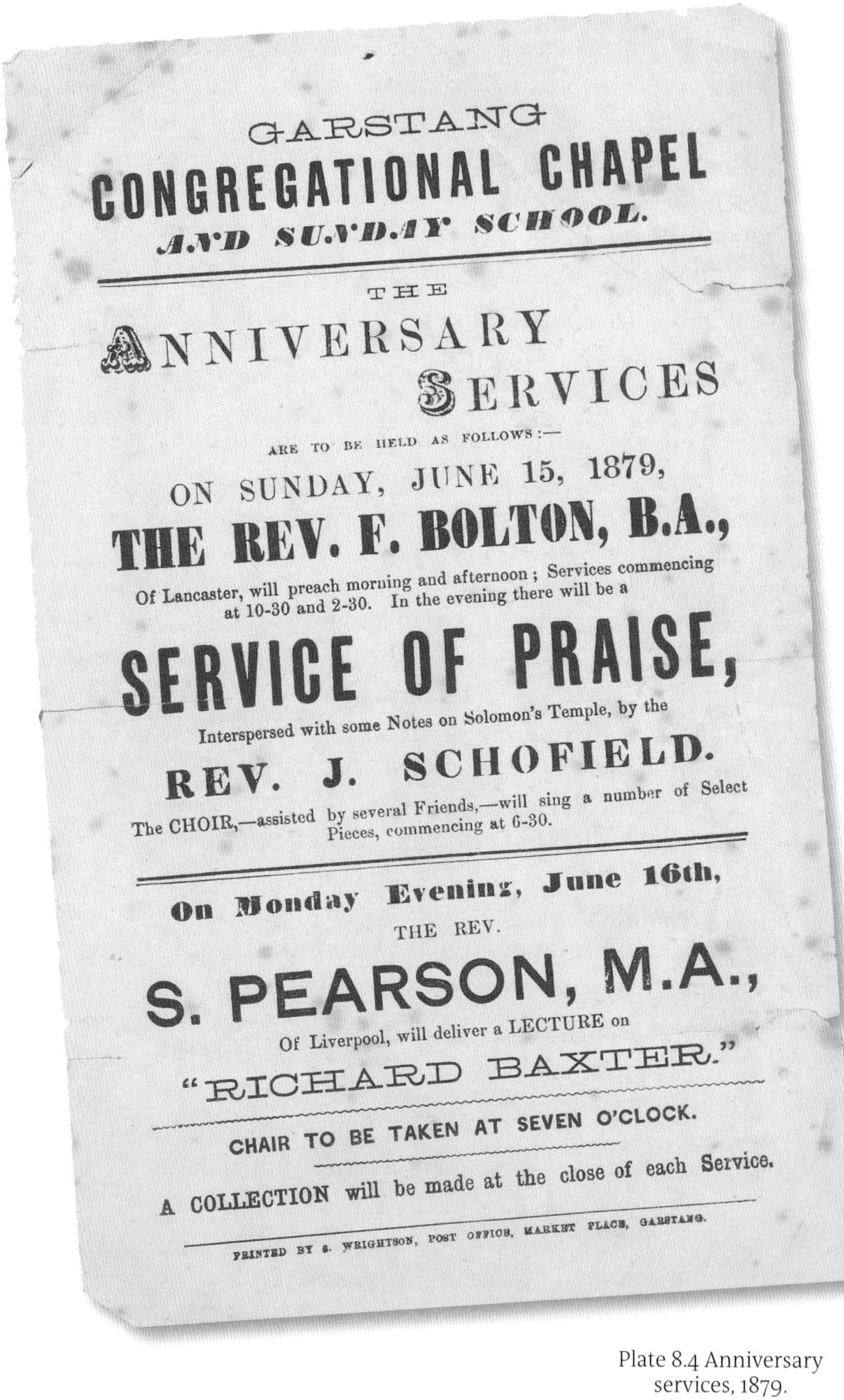

GARSTANG
CONGREGATIONAL CHAPEL
AND SUNDAY SCHOOL.

THE
ANNIVERSARY SERVICES

ARE TO BE HELD AS FOLLOWS:—

ON SUNDAY, JUNE 15, 1879,

THE REV. F. BOLTON, B.A.,

Of Lancaster, will preach morning and afternoon; Services commencing at 10-30 and 2-30. In the evening there will be a

SERVICE OF PRAISE,

Interspersed with some Notes on Solomon's Temple, by the

REV. J. SCHOFIELD.

The CHOIR,—assisted by several Friends,—will sing a number of Select Pieces, commencing at 6-30.

On Monday Evening, June 16th,

THE REV.

S. PEARSON, M.A.,

Of Liverpool, will deliver a LECTURE on

"RICHARD BAXTER."

CHAIR TO BE TAKEN AT SEVEN O'CLOCK.

A COLLECTION will be made at the close of each Service.

PRINTED BY S. WRIGHTSON, POST OFFICE, MARKET PLACE, GARSTANG.

Plate 8.4 Anniversary services, 1879.

top of Ball Brow (now called Bridge Street). After travelling by wagonette they ate at Winbold House, Knot[t] End, where a dinner cost 1*s*. 3*d*. and a tea 6*d*. Plate 8.5 shows some details from the Sunday School Treat, 1895.

During 1879 Revd Schofield, much hindered by bodily weaknesses and other causes, gave notice of his intention to resign.[30] By July of that year suitable candidates for the pastorate were being discussed at church meetings. (By this time the chapel had begun to be called church.) Revd Schofield resigned in November 1879 and retired to Lytham.[31]

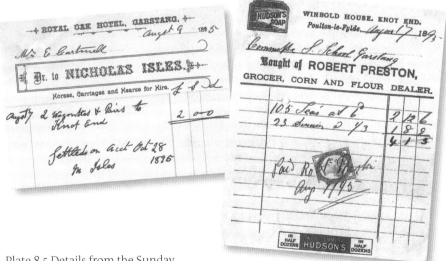

Plate 8.5 Details from the Sunday School Treat, 1895

• CHAPTER NINE •

An uneasy ministry

T HE LANCASHIRE CONGREGATIONAL UNION recommended a restruc-
turing of the way the church was run as it had operated without deacons
for several years. A church meeting, held in April 1880, voted to appoint four
deacons: Edward Cartmell of Garstang, Henry Smith of Bowgreave, James
Clark of Pilling and Robert Gardner of Garstang.[1] Edward Cartmell, secretary,
and Henry Smith, treasurer, were already officers of the church.

In July 1880 the Revd Joseph Cockram, of Tyldesley, near Wigan, was
invited to become the church's minister from September of that year
(Plate 9.1).[2] There must have been some doubt as to his suitability since he
was offered only a one year appointment, but was promised an extension of
this appointment if his ministry proved satisfactory. His stipend was to be
£100 per annum and he was to be allowed four weeks annual leave.[3]

He began his ministry in earnest: Bible classes for young men were
held on Sunday afternoons; an elementary singing class was established
and occasional week night services were held at Barnacre and Catterall.[4] A
public tea meeting took place later that year to welcome him to the pastorate
(Plate 9.2).[5] In September 1880 there were 19 church members (Plate 9.3) plus
many adherants.

Trouble started in the latter part of 1880. The Revd Cockram, a learned
man, placed much emphasis on the Old Testament. He introduced the
chanting of the Psalms, and chant books were purchased for the choir and
congregation.[6] Many members did not like this change of emphasis and

Milton G. Wilde
34, TALBOT ROAD
BLACKPOOL

Left: Plate 9.1 The Reverend Joseph Cockram and below, Plate 9.2, a poster for a tea meeting to welcome him.[26]

within a few months people had started to desert the church, pews began to empty and, consequently, church income fell.

In January 1881, James Clark, one of the deacons who had been an enthusiastic supporter of the church, began to write a series of acrimonious letters to the church secretary. He said from henceforth he and his wife would sever their links with the church and would not give any financial assistance because of the Revd Cockram's style of ministry. He accused both Edward Cartmell and Henry Smith of agreeing with the Revd Cockram to change the form of worship without consulting the congregation. He said he had been told that Edward Cartmell and his brothers, in an alliance with the Revd Cockram, had wanted the form of service changed. He reminded Mr Cartmell of a comment made when Dr Bell's family left Garstang: 'A place of worship does not get on so well when ruled by one family.' He ended his letters by saying that, in his opinion, the New Testament and not the Old should be the Christian's guide.[7] James Clark ceased to attend the church and, as he had not returned by January 1882, was replaced as deacon by George Whittaker of Kirkland.[8]

A meeting of seat holders and adult members of the choir was held at the close of morning service on Sunday 22nd May 1881 to discuss the desirability, or otherwise, of continuing with the use of Dr Allon's Chant Book. The Revd Cockram pleaded with them to give more consideration to the Psalms, but the recommendation of the meeting was that for the next six months the chants should

Plate 9.3 Church Members, 1880.

1880	ROLL OF CHURCH MEMBERS.					
CHRISTIAN AND SURNAME.	Age.	RESIDENCE.	OCCUPATION.	DATE OF ADMISSION. Month. Year.		
Joseph Cockram	1	The Manse	Minister	Sept 1	1880
Thomas Smith	2	Rose Mount	Gentleman		
James Clark	3	South Field	Farmer		
Mrs Clark	4	"	"		
William Dobson	5	Barnacre	"		
Mrs Fisher	7	Claughton			
John Cartmell	6	Bonds	Grocer		
Mrs James	8	Garstang			
Miss James	9	"	S. Principal		
John Hamer	10	Bonds	Gentleman		
Mrs Hamer	11	"			
Henry Smith	12	Bowgreave	Agent		
Mrs Smith	13	"			
Robert Singleton	14	Kirkland	Farmer		
George Whittaker	15	"	"		
Edward Cartmell	16	Garstang	Draper		
Mrs Rigby	17	Barnacre	Farmer		
Mrs Cockram	18	The Manse			
Robert Gardner	19	Garstang	Bootmaker		
Miss Mary Stephenson	20	Garstang	Servant	April 4	1881

be discontinued during morning service: they could, however, be used occasionally in the afternoon at the discretion of the minister.[9]

The following month the Revd Cockram tendered his resignation to take effect from September 1881, exactly one year after starting his ministry; his reason being the bitterness which had arisen between some members of the congregation and himself.[10] In his letter of resignation he said:

> Pews are now emptied of those who but a short time since appeared to be earnest supporters of the work. I hope and pray that my removal may be the means of restoring that calm and quiet that has been disturbed by my misunderstood efforts.

The church was short of money, possibly owing to the fact that many people had left. In July 1881, Robert Mansergh, a representative of the Lancashire Congregational Union, suggested 'the Forton folk' might agree to group the two churches together and share a minister.[11] Whether or not discussions took place is not known, but the union of the two churches did not take place.

The Revd Cockram's resignation was quickly followed by that of Robert Cartmell, the harmonist and choir leader. He favoured the Revd Cockram's style of ministry, and in his letter of resignation said, 'I have no desire to experience the same treatment that our excellent and worthy pastor has received.'[12]

At an extraordinary church meeting held shortly afterwards the congregation was reluctant to accept the Revd Cockram's resignation and encouraged him to stay another year. They were unable to guarantee him a fixed stipend. The terms were that he would be given the Congregational Union grant of £40, the grant of £10 from Lady Hewley's trustees, the rent of £20 for the manse and the church would give him whatever it could afford after all other expenses had been paid. A testimonial, signed by many members of the congregation, was presented to him and this led to the withdrawal of his resignation and his acceptance of the proposed conditions.[13] In his letter of acceptance he said that people should give more willingly to the finances of the church, 'Giving to the Lord's treasury as if in his sight.' He wished the congregation to be reminded of the Divine rule, 'They that preach the gospel should live by the gospel.'[14]

Plate 9.4 Band of Hope and Temperance Society Pledge Card

Robert Cartmell must have been persuaded to continue as harmonist as records show he was paid a fee of 10s. 0d. per annum until he officially retired in November 1893.[15]

In November 1881, the Revd Cockram was instrumental in forming the Garstang Congregational Band of Hope and Temperance Society.[16] Officers of the society were: Revd J Cockram (president), R Gardner (treasurer) and R Cartmell (secretary). Members of the committee were George Whittaker, Wm Rigby, Wm Robinson, E Cartmell, Revd T Hamer, Revd E Le Mare and Mrs R Cartmell. The pledge taken by all members was:

> By divine assistance I will abstain from all intoxicating drinks as beverages and discountenance all the causes and practices of intemperance (Plate 9.4).[17]

Between November 1881 and the following March a total of 86 people signed the pledge. Meetings of the society took place monthly and were held in

Plate 9.5 Church Poster

the Grammar school. There was usually an address concerning the evils of alcohol followed by some form of entertainment: people sang or recited poetry and there were frequent lantern shows. Children were encouraged to bring their friends and prizes were given to those who introduced most new members.[18] In July 1882 a petition signed by 48 members of the congregation was presented to the House of Commons by the Rt Hon F A Stanley MP in favour of the closure of public houses on Sundays.[19] It was unsuccessful.

Until that time wine, containing alcohol, had been served at Holy Communion, then referred to as the Ordinance of the Lord's Supper. At a church meeting it was resolved that this should be substituted by unfermented wine.[20] Church members were expected to attend the Ordinance of the Lord's Supper held once a month. A register of communicants was kept and absences noted.

A poster dated 1882 states that the Lord's Supper was held on the first Sunday afternoon of each month. The poster (Plate 9.5) gives information about events taking place at church and names some office holders. (It may have been fastened to the notice board outside the church.)

In March 1882 the grant from the Lancashire Congregational Union was cut to £25 and the church was told that the grant would cease the following year. This meant the church was no longer in a position to offer the Revd Cockram the stipend agreed previously, and he felt compelled to resign from September of that year. When the time came for his resignation to take effect he had been unsuccessful in obtaining another pastorate, so the church agreed to him preaching at the church as often as he was able for the rest of the year and, if funds would allow, he would be paid £1 per Sunday.[21]

Church finances were not healthy and seat holders were urged to pay up by the end of the quarter. By the end of December 1882 they were compelled to call upon lay preachers as they could no longer afford to pay visiting ministers.[22] In February 1883, at the request of the Lancashire Congregational Union, a proposition was put to seat holders and members of the church regarding the unification of the churches at Garstang and Forton under one pastorate. The motion was carried, with only one person voting against it.[23] The members at Forton, however, decided it was not desirable for their church to enter into a joint pastorate with Garstang, so the union did not proceed.[24]

After the departure of the Revd Cockram, James Clark and his wife returned to the church and were readmitted to membership. He immediately immersed himself in the life of the church, chairing meetings, auditing accounts and being re-elected deacon in November 1884 when Henry Smith moved away.[25]

In 1889 the Revd Cockram was appointed to the pastorate of Little Asby, near Kirkby Stephen in Westmoreland, where he had a successful ministry (Plate 9.6).[26] He remained there until he died. In 1900 an urgent appeal was made by the Lancashire Congregational Union to the Garstang Church on behalf of his widow and daughter. The Revd Cockram had died from a lengthy and painful illness. His widow had been left totally unprovided for and there were heavy doctor's bills to pay. (There was no National Health Service or pension for old people.) It was his daughter's wish to move into a town where she would be able to take in lodgers to support herself and her mother, and pay the doctor's bills. Their removal to town required money, which they did not possess, and the church was asked to make an urgent donation.[27] It was decided that a box should be placed in the church porch for voluntary donations, but it is not known how much was collected.

Plate 9.6 The Reverend Joseph Cockram, his Wife, Daughter and Grand-daughter, outside Little Asby Church.

• CHAPTER TEN •

The interregnum 1883–1888

T HE DEPARTURE OF THE REVEREND COCKRAM led to the church
being without a resident minister for five years, and its reliance on lay
preachers and visiting ministers. It was fortunate that during that time both
the Revd Thomas Hamer and his brother-in-law, the Revd Ebenezer Le Mare,
lived in the Garstang area and gave support to the church.

The Revd Thomas Hamer and his sister, Sarah Jane (Sallie), together with
other brothers and sisters, were born at Scorton, the children of John and
Margaret Hamer. At that time their father, a groom, was employed by George
Fishwick Esq. of Scorton, a cotton spinner.[1] In the 1840s George Fishwick
often presided at meetings held at Garstang Independent Chapel to support
the work of the London Missionary Society (LMS).[2] The Hamers were staunch
church workers. In the 1870s John Hamer was chapel keeper, grave digger and
provider of transport when Congregational Union representatives visited the
church.[3] By the 1880s John Hamer and his wife had moved to Bonds and lived
in a cottage in Jackson Terrace, at the bottom of Bowgreave hill (Plate 10.1).[4]

In 1867 Ebenezer Le Mare, aged 19, enrolled at Lancashire Independent
College, Manchester, a training college for Congregational ministers. He was
accepted as a missionary by the LMS and arrived in Madras, India, in 1873.
He married Sarah Jane (Sallie) Hamer on 24th November 1875 in Davidson
Street Congregational Church, Madras. Sallie had trained as a teacher, and
was also an artist, pianist and singer. Ebenezer was a missionary in southern
India for nearly 20 years and most of their children were born there.[5, 6] One

Plate 10.1 Jackson Terrace, also known as Jackson Row.

of their children died when they were on a visit to England. The church burial register records that Cyril Hamer Le Mare, a missionary's child, died on October 18th 1882 aged 22 months. The tombstone in the churchyard records that he was their fourth child and was born at Salem in southern India. The Revd Le Mare was a frequent visitor to the church during 1882 and 1883, and again in 1887 and 1888. He encouraged the church to support the work of the LMS, particularly the fund for widows and orphans of deceased missionaries.[7] It became a tradition for many years to hold a collection for this fund at the Communion service held on the first Sunday in January each year. The Revd Le Mare and his wife were church members for a short time and he occasionally took church services.[8] In 1882 their children, Percy and Amy, began attending Sunday school.[9] It is possible they had come to Garstang to help look after Sallie's parents, John and Margaret Hamer, who were getting old and failing in health. In December 1883 the Le Mare family left Garstang for missionary work in India.[10]

At the same time the Revd Thomas Hamer and his wife, formerly Miss Mary Bell, together with their two daughters came to reside at Bonds and stayed for almost three years. The Revd Hamer devoted much of his time

Plate 10.2 Band of Hope and Temperance Society entertainment evening.

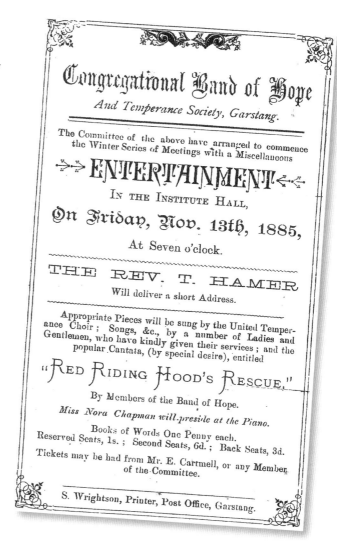

Plate 10.2 Band of Hope and Temperance Society entertainment evening.

to the work of the church. He frequently took services, officiated at Holy Communion, chaired church meetings and supported the Band of Hope and Temperance Society (Plate 10.2). The height of the Temperance Society's popularity was in 1885 when it had 183 members, probably drawn from all churches in Garstang.[11] It was with much regret that the church bade farewell to the family in September 1886 when the Revd Hamer accepted the pastorate of the church at Little Lever, near Bolton.[12]

However, he was invited back to Garstang to take the Sunday school anniversary services held the first Sunday following Queen Victoria's Golden Jubilee (20th June 1887). The afternoon service was based on 1 Peter 2:17, 'Love all men. Fear God. Honour the king'. Both services had a Jubilee theme. He paid tribute to the Queen for her constitutional government of the country,

Plate 10.3 Photo of the Independent Chapel taken between 1867 and 1885.

ascribing much of the government to the influence and wise counsel of the late Prince Consort.[13, 14]

General maintenance continued. In 1884 Messrs Collinson and sons decorated the school room (now used as the vestry), painted the windows, grained and varnished the doors. Edward Cartmell supplied new blinds and cords for the windows.[15] The porch, built in 1867 over part of the old graveyard, had started to drift away from the church; subsidence may have been the cause of the problem. In the winter of 1885 iron bolts were put through the porch to hold it together and to hold it to the church. Ivy was planted around both the church and the porch.[16] Plate 10.3 shows the church between 1867 and 1885 and Plate 10.4 shows the bolts which are still in place today.

Dampness in church was a recurring problem. George Whittaker and Edward Cartmell met with Messrs Collinson and sons of Nateby to discuss the best way of ventilating the church and the installation of a new stove.[17] Later reports, however, showed that dampness was a continuing problem.

Coal and oil for heating and lighting were purchased from Jonathan Jowitt Thomas, a pharmacist in Garstang and member of the church. He audited the church accounts for many years.[18, 19] He was a trustee of the manse and served on the church management committee. Benjamin Fisher, the chapel keeper (caretaker), asked for an increase in salary because of his increased duties. The committee decided to increase his salary from £3 to £4 per annum.[20] His duties included attending to heating in church, stoking up fires in the schoolroom, trimming lamps and generally looking after the premises. He was paid extra for sweeping the chimney and for any duties in the graveyard. A thermometer was purchased for the church.[21] (Did this mean that members thought the church was not being kept warm enough, or had the deacons been complaining that too much fuel was being used?) There was also a toilet to attend to. A new door was fitted to the chapel 'closet' and in December 1883 Richard Nicholson was asked to replace the slates that had blown off the closet roof during recent storms.[22, 23]

In September 1883 Garstang Church decided to hold a Harvest Thanksgiving service and the ladies were invited to decorate the church.[24] This, the first Harvest Festival to be held in the church, was to become an annual event. A newspaper report stated:

> The decoration and display of grains, flowers and fruit were exquisite. In the porch were bunches of wheat while at the ends of each pew was a bouquet, and on each window sill a wreath of flowers. Before the pulpit were sheaves of wheat and rye, and on the communion table clusters of grapes and various kinds of flowers, fruit and plants were placed.

The preacher, the Revd J T Camm of Blackpool, took his morning sermon from Isaiah 4:3, 'The joy in harvest', and in the afternoon from Exodus 23:16, 'Keep the feast of the harvest'. There were large congregations at both services.[25, 26]

The Le Mare family returned to Garstang in 1886 and stayed until 1888

Plate 10.4 Porch showing Iron Bolts to hold its Walls together and to secure it to the Church.
(Photo 2003)

Plate 10.5
The Reverend Ebenezer Le Mare.

when John Hamer died of paralysis, aged 84 years.[27] Following John's death his widow, Margaret, went to live with her son Thomas and family at Little Lever. When the Revd Le Mare retired from missionary work he and his wife started a school in Fleetwood.[28] Following the closure of the school Sallie ran a boarding house, helped by her daughters, Amy and Connie. Ebenezer became a school attendance officer working for the County Council. The family were members of Fleetwood Congregational Church where Ebenezer became a deacon (Plate 10.5). It is recorded that he always attended church social events 'resplendent in a velvet smoking jacket and skull cap'.[29] He died in 1939 aged 90 and is buried in the church yard at Garstang. Plate 10.6 shows the relationship between the Bell, McGilchrist, Hamer and Le Mare families.

Plate 10.6. Relationship between the Bell, McGilchrist, Hamer and Le Mare families. Those indicated by a * are buried in the churchyard to the west of the church.

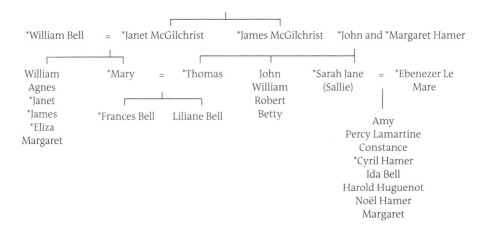

• CHAPTER ELEVEN •

Renovation and restoration 1890

THE REVEREND WILLIAM JEFFCOAT BURMAN became minister of Garstang Congregational Church in November 1888.[1] He preferred to live in lodgings rather than the manse as he was a widower. The 1891 census shows him lodging with Thomas Smith and wife at Beechmount, High Street, Garstang (Plate 11.1). He stayed just less than three years, but it was a time of much activity.

Two services were held each Sunday, and a third during the week. However, summer week night services were discontinued in 1890 as many members of the congregation lived long distances from church and most were engaged in agriculture.[2] Church meetings were held quarterly and the Band of Hope continued to meet monthly in the Grammar school.[3] In 1890 services re-commenced in a cottage in Barnacre and were much appreciated by the old and infirm of that neighbourhood.[4]

Urgent repairs were needed as the church had fallen into a dilapidated state with water pouring into the building from above and seeping up from below.[5] In 1891 it was referred to as the Old Chapel under the leadership of Mr Burman.[6] Shortly before it was renovated the Revd B Nightingale visited the church and made the following observations:

> A patent padlock, which requires much patience and careful manip-ulation, keeps the little iron gate closed against all intruders. A porch faces the road, which is quite a modern addition, on the left of which is the 'way in'. A sort of vestibule is formed by a wooden

Plate 11.1 Number 2 Beechmount (left of picture), High Street, Garstang. (Photo 2014)

screen, which runs nearly the whole width of the chapel. This will be found, near the floor, to be blistered and scorched terribly, and the explanation is that a vigorous heating apparatus is immediately beneath. Nobody, however, complains, for the Garstang friends like warmth of more kinds than one.

David Watson, a member of the church involved in the church restoration of 1984, said the remains of a fire grate were unearthed in the porch, and a coal cellar was discovered under the stairs. A heating system akin to that of Roman times was found under the church floor. Heat from the fire would have circulated under the floor which was supported on a series of soot-blackened pillars about two feet in height. A chimney on the roof is the only evidence remaining of that primitive, but probably highly effective, heating system. Nightingale continued:

Two aisles run down the wall sides, and between are the pews - like parallels of latitude - eight in number, open at both ends, and divided irregularly by pieces of board. The pulpit, or rather the plat-form is in front, to the right of which is the miniature singing pew, and to the left a large square pew - the only relic left within of the

Plate 11.2 The Liberal Club (on right), Bridge Street, Garstang. (Photo 1905)

past, and it is set aside for the minister. Its appearance suggests that he at least is expected to be a family man. On this side is a door leading into a room behind, which serves both as vestry and Sunday school, and above that again is another room, of exactly the same size, used now for storage purposes...Over the doorway is a little gallery... The roof is unceiled, and so the building has a somewhat barn-like appearance inside. The walls are the original ones, and they are all that is left of the old building.[7]

A renovation committee was appointed namely Mr Burman, John Cartmell, Robert Cartmell, Mr Crossley and Mr Benson.[8] Robert Gardner and Edward Cartmell were appointed collectors and each was given a subscription book in which to record donations. Written in the front of each was a statement which concluded:

...The congregation has promised a large proportion of the estimated cost. They, however, need and earnestly ask the help of friends outside. Contributions will be thankfully received.[9]

The largest donation was given by Mr James Williamson, the Liberal Member of Parliament for the Lancaster Area, who contributed £20. He had opened the Garstang and District Liberal Club in Bridge Street (Plate 11.2) in February 1889 and had been made very welcome by enthusiastic Liberal supporters, including Edward Cartmell, the church secretary.[10] Several members of the congregation made donations ranging from 1s. 0d. to £5. In total £100 was collected.

Mr E Howard Dawson, architect, of Lancaster, surveyed the church and its immediate surroundings, and put forward suggestions for its repair.[11] Renovations were carried out in the Spring of 1890 and took a total of six weeks. During this time services were held in the Assembly rooms at the Liberal club at a rental of 5s. 0d. per week for the premises, plus an extra 2s. 6d. for the services of the steward, Moses Cartmell.[12]

When the church was renovated in 1867 it was entirely re-seated, but at that time members requested that two of the old style square pews of the high backed, loose-box fashion should remain. These were removed in the 1890 renovation and substituted by open pews. The pews were stained dark brown and varnished, the ventilation improved, the platform at the front of the church altered and a new door constructed to the vestry.[13] In the small gallery at the rear of the church the pews were altered; each had its own small door and the seats were made more comfortable. A local newspaper described the interior of the church in detail:

> The roof of the chapel has been coloured in pleasing shades of blue and cream, and the roof timbers cleaned. The walls have been divided by several horizontal ivory-coloured bands, decorated and enclosed by dark lines, and the spaces between the bands have been painted in several warm tones of colour, from rich cream at the top to a warm terracotta at the base. The walls are further deco-rated with several medallions painted between the windows. On the window splays there is a conventionalised treatment of the lily, painted in a soft tone of russet green. The wall behind the platform has been more elaborately treated with ribbon scrolls, and rose and ashlar diaper patterns. In the centre of the wall are three circular headed panels, the middle one containing a conventionalised treat-ment of the wheat and the vine.[14]

The elaborate decoration described above was typical of style during the Victorian era. The woodwork was painted both inside and out, and the exte-rior walls of the chapel and boundary walls pointed with cement. The flags on the pathway around the building were replaced by asphalt. The main contractors were: R Nicholson of Barnacre (masonry and plastering); Mr Helm of Barnacre (carpentry); R Bennet of Manchester (decorations); and

Edward Cartmell (linoleum, carpeting and window blinds). The cost of the renovation was £135 5s. 3d.[15]

John Cartmell made a gift to the church of umbrella stands at the ends of each pew and Mrs Crossley gave a stone font.[16] Mr Staveley was paid £2 10s. 0d. for repairing the harmonium.[17]

The reopening service was held in the church on Saturday 25th April at 3pm followed by refreshments in the assembly rooms of the Liberal club where 150 people sat down to tea. This was followed by a meeting in church, presided over by Edward B Dawson J.P. of Lancaster who said, 'It is difficult to recognise in this building the Garstang Chapel of previous years'.[18] There were several speakers. The Revd P Webster of Forton said that the backbone of Nonconformity was made up of people such as deacons and teachers, who carried on with work in the churches, though ministers might constantly change. Robert Mansergh of Lancaster, secretary of the Preston district of the Congregational Union, spoke of the advisability of a congregation co-operating heartily with their minister. He said that without such unity of action the good accomplished would be comparatively small. Celebrations continued on the Sunday and over the two days £27 10s. 0d. was collected. This almost extinguished the debt on the outlay for renovation.[19]

In April the following year (1891) the congregation was urged to contribute more as church funds were £6 10s. 0d. in debt. The dampness, unfortunately, had not been cured by the improved ventilation and, following a spell of damp weather, patches of mould had begun to appear on the walls.[20]

On April 22nd 1891 the Revd Burman announced he was leaving to undertake the pastorate of a new church at Grange-over-Sands. Edward Cartmell presented him with an illuminated address at a tea meeting held to bid him farewell.[21]

• CHAPTER TWELVE •

The close of the 19th century

THE REVEREND JOHN JAMES WILLIAMS, a talented musician, became the ninth minister of Garstang Congregational Church in December 1891, with a stipend of £100 per annum (Plate 12.1).[1,2]

In 1893 the congregation began grumbling about sounds coming from the old harmonium. Edward Cartmell decided to purchase an organ being advertised by Over Wyresdale Church and to donate it to the Congregational Church.[3,4] The cost of the organ was £5 and John Helme, carrier, charged 10s. 0d. for transporting it to Garstang.[5] Henry Ainscough of the Organ Works, Preston, inspected the organ and described it as having one manual and an independent pedal organ. It had seven organ pipes between 2 and 16 foot in length, some made of wood and some of metal, and the case was of a suitable design for the church. His estimate for cleaning and repairing the organ, and erecting it in church was £5 10s. 0d.[6,7]

To celebrate the installation of the organ a concert was held. The Revd Williams gave an address on music and a choir from Preston sang, accompanied by Mr J S Greenwood on the organ.[8] Robert Cartmell, who had played the harmonium for 21 years, resigned when the new organ was installed, his place being taken by his nephew, William Harold Cartmell. Frank Fisher volunteered to be organ blower and was given a gratuity of 10s. 0d. per annum.[9]

Dampness in church was a problem, so a paraffin stove was purchased in an attempt to keep the organ dry, alas without success.[10] Shortly afterwards it

Plate 12.1 The Revd John James Williams

was decided that, as the organ was being ruined by dampness on the ground floor, an organ loft and singing gallery should be constructed over the Sunday school (vestry). The Revd Williams, Edward Cartmell and his brother, John, were appointed to oversee the work.[11] Richard Heathcote (Edward Cartmell's uncle), a builder and joiner from Preston, drew up plans and specifications for the alterations.[12] An archway was made through the wall and an organ loft and singing gallery were constructed. More stops were added to the organ and it was moved from the body of the church into its new lofty position.[13] In September 1895 special services were held to celebrate the opening of the new organ chamber, choir gallery and relocated organ. A celebration tea was held in the Liberal Assembly Rooms, after which an adjournment was made to the church where a large congregation assembled. The organist and choir of High Street Chapel, Lancaster, provided the music and the address was given by their pastor, the Revd J F Cowley.[14]

In 1890 there was widespread concern regarding the increasing number of men being enlisted into the armed forces across Europe. In July 1890 a Universal Peace Congress was called in London to consider the fact that countries were competing against each other in the race to be ready for the

next war. One of the speakers, Dr Brooke Westcott, Bishop of Durham (Plate 12.2),[15] invited churches everywhere to devote the Sunday before Christmas each year to the cause of peace. Services were to be based on the song of the angels (Luke 2:14), '...and on earth peace, goodwill toward men.[16, 17, 18]

In December of that year 102 churches in Lancaster and district designated that Sunday as Peace Sunday. Several

Plate 12.2 Dr Brooke Westcott, Bishop of Durham

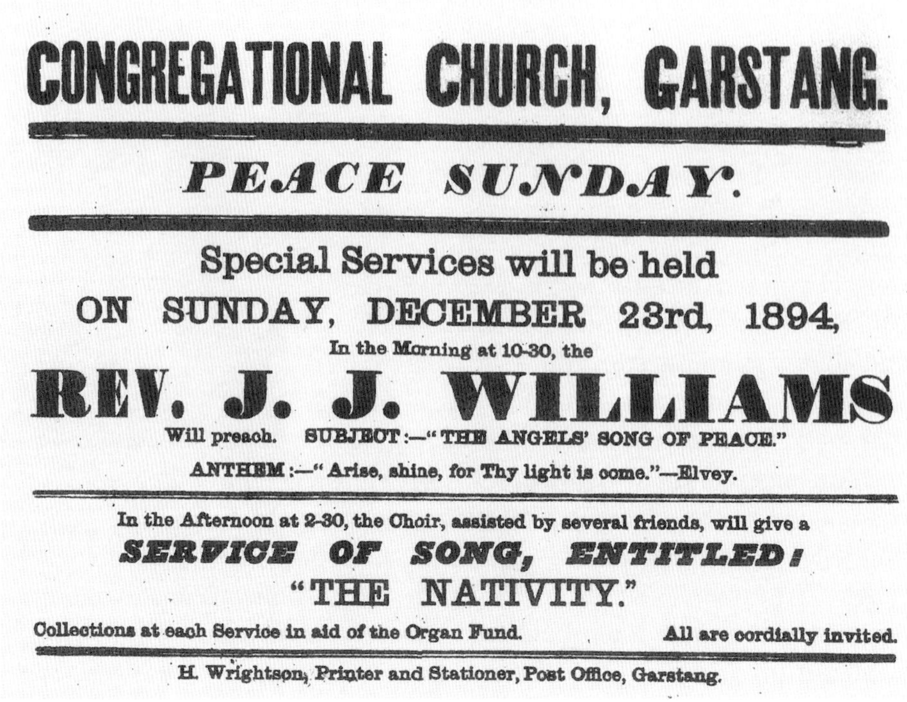

Plate 12.3 Peace Sunday Poster, 1894

ministers based their sermon on Isaiah 2:4, '...they shall beat their swords into ploughshares and their spears into pruning hooks: nation shall not lift up sword against nation, neither shall they learn war any more.'

However, it was not until 1894 that Peace Sunday was celebrated at Garstang Congregational Church (Plate 12.3). The Revd Williams, encouraged by the large congregations, said he hoped it would become an annual event.[19]

During the latter part of 1894 the Congregationalists and Wesleyans of Garstang began holding joint Sunday evening services fortnightly, with the Methodist minister preaching at the Congregational Church and the Revd Williams preaching at the Wesleyan Chapel.[20]

In 1896 the Revd Williams decided to retire from the ministry owing to his advancing years and increasing infirmity.[21] It was almost a year before the next minister, the Revd John Angell-Jones BA, of Manchester was appointed.[22]

As there had been substantial building alterations the church needed decorating. Design specifications and estimates were obtained. The building committee laid down specifications of their own: the ceiling was to be pale cream and only two colours to be allowed on the side walls. The wall at the pulpit end was to be treated separately and it was to be 'distinct' in style.[23]

The design of Mr R W Lang of Garstang, which included a frieze around the top of the walls was chosen, but it was decided that the organ pipes should be decorated in a manner similar to those on another design. Messrs Collinson and son of Nateby were awarded the contract for the decorating.[24] Miss Lizzie Swarbrick, John Cartmell's niece, offered to decorate the panels in front of the singing gallery and her offer was accepted with thanks.[25]

June 1897 was a special month in the life of the church, the town and the country. The beginning of the month saw the half-yearly rent audit for Garstang being paid directly to the owner, Bertram William Arnold Keppel, Esq. It was the first time in over a century that the rent had been received by the owner. (The Keppels had been absentee landlords.) Bertram W A Keppel inherited Garstang when he was only 13 years old, and had attained his majority on January 12th 1897. During his minority the estate, having been in Chancery, had been administered by trustees.[26, 27, 28]

On Monday, 9th June, the Whitsuntide festivities took place. The Preston Guardian, 12 June 1897, reported:

> The thoroughfares were thronged by the inhabitants and people from neighbouring villages: banners, bannerettes and bunting, among which the Union Jack was greatly in evidence, were visible everywhere, and music filled the air. The fairground was fully occupied by roundabouts and the usual accompaniments which come under the comprehensive head of, 'fun of the fair'. The Oddfellows processions are held alternately at Churchtown and Garstang, and this year the members of the Loyal Adelaide Lodge, Garstang district, were called upon to don the regalia. After service at St Thomas's Church, conducted by the vicar, The Rev. G. B. Stones, the members assumed marching order, and, headed by their banner and Carnforth Brass Band, they joined the general procession, which included children from the various schools. The general procession was headed by Poulton Brass Band. Catholic, Church of England, Wesleyan and Congregational places of worship were largely represented.

Less than two weeks later the town was once more in joyful mood as it celebrated the Diamond Jubilee of Queen Victoria. Celebrations began on Sunday, 20th June, when the Queen, together with family members, took part in a simple ceremony of thanksgiving at St George's Chapel, Windsor. The ceremony featured the specially commissioned Jubilee hymn, 'O King of Kings, whose reign of old hath been from everlasting'. It was written by the Bishop of Wakefield and set to music by Sir Arthur Sullivan (better known as half of

EXORS. OF THE LATE

MRS. ROBERT GARDNER,

Boot & Shoe Maker,

Have a nice selection of Ladies', Gent's & Children's Boots and Shoes for Autumn and Winter wear.

Also Ladies' and Gent's Shoes and Slippers for evening wear.

Hand-sewn Boots & Shoes made to order.

Repairs neatly and promptly executed on the premises.

Bridge Street, GARSTANG.

(Opposite the Post Office.)

ESTABLISHED 1810.

W. & S. CARR,

PRACTICAL

Watch and Clock Makers,

Jewellers, &c

Splendid selection of Ladies' Watches from 10/6. Gent's from 6/-.

All patterns of Clocks from 1/6 to £4.

Gold and Silver Brooches, Spectacles, Accordians.

Wedding, Keeper and Engagement Rings at all prices.

To each purchaser of our Guinea Gold Wedding Rings a suitable present will be given.

Repairs promptly attended to in town or country.

Plate 12.4 Selection of Tradesmen's half page Adverts, Bazaar Booklet, 1897

JAMES S. STOREY,

General Furnishing Ironmonger

Oil Merchant, &c.

Market Place, Garstang

Ammunition, Fire Ranges, Iron Pig Troughs, Trunks, Iron Bedsteads, Mattresses.

Lamps in great variety.

Agent for Taylor & Wilson's Wringing & Washing Machines.

Roofing Felt, Wire Netting, Barb Wire, and Galvanized Corrugated Iron Roofing.

Large quantities of these always in stock.

Every description of Burning and Lubricating Oils.

30

Wm. Harrison,

SADDLER,

Harness & Collar Maker,

Church Street, Garstang.

Harness made to order from Holden's best oak bark tanned leather.

Repairs neatly and promptly attended to.

Agent for Hutton's Poultry Balm and Condition Paste.

28

Market Place

Refreshment Rooms

For a Cup of Good Tea or Coffee, Hot Pies and Sandwiches.

Richard Bartlett,

Family Grocer & Bread Baker,

High Street & Market Place,

GARSTANG.

30

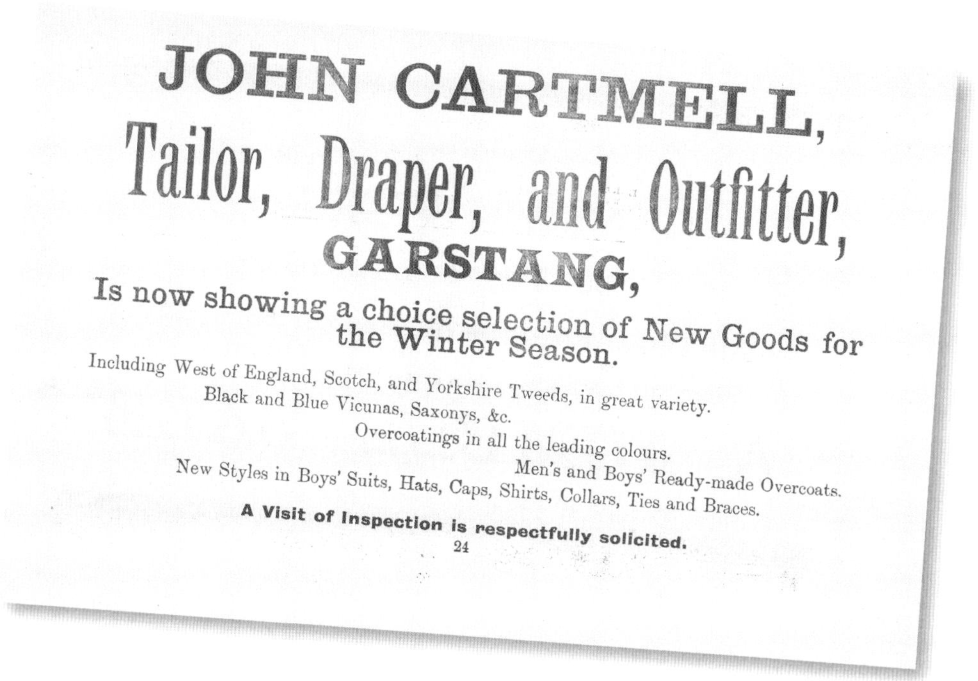

JOHN CARTMELL,
Tailor, Draper, and Outfitter,
GARSTANG,

Is now showing a choice selection of New Goods for the Winter Season.

Including West of England, Scotch, and Yorkshire Tweeds, in great variety.
Black and Blue Vicunas, Saxonys, &c.

Overcoatings in all the leading colours.

Men's and Boys' Ready-made Overcoats.

New Styles in Boys' Suits, Hats, Caps, Shirts, Collars, Ties and Braces.

A Visit of Inspection is respectfully solicited.

24

Plate 12.5 Selection of
Tradesmen's full page Adverts,
Bazaar Booklet, 1897.

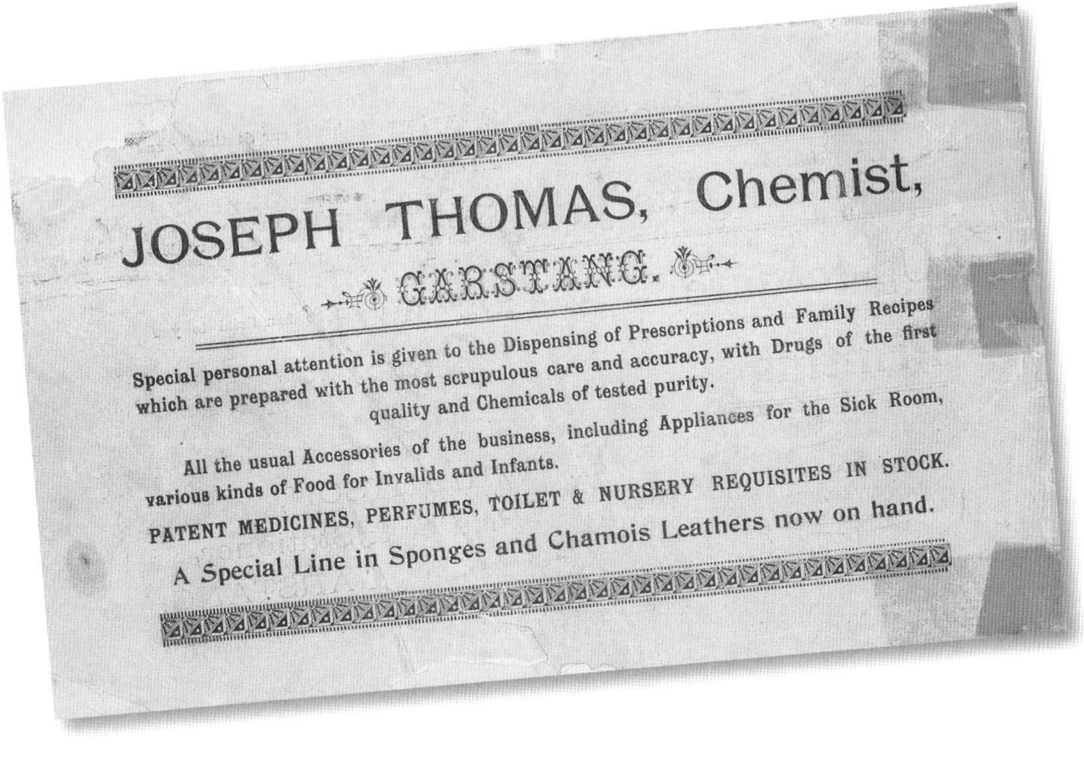

JOSEPH THOMAS, Chemist,
GARSTANG.

Special personal attention is given to the Dispensing of Prescriptions and Family Recipes which are prepared with the most scrupulous care and accuracy, with Drugs of the first quality and Chemicals of tested purity.

All the usual Accessories of the business, including Appliances for the Sick Room, various kinds of Food for Invalids and Infants.

PATENT MEDICINES, PERFUMES, TOILET & NURSERY REQUISITES IN STOCK.

A Special Line in Sponges and Chamois Leathers now on hand.

the Gilbert and Sullivan duo). He named the tune Bishopgate. The hymn was appointed to be sung on that Sunday in all churches and chapels throughout Britain. Celebrations continued the following Tuesday, 22nd June, with a service at St Paul's Cathedral. The ceremony included the singing of the 'Te Deum Laudamus' (We Praise thee O God) and the National Anthem.[29, 30, 31]

Garstang Congregational Church decided to hold its Sunday school anniversary on Queen Victoria's Diamond Jubilee Sunday. The Revd J Angell-Jones, the newly appointed minister, preached in the morning. The Revd J J Williams, the previous minister, took the service in the evening and gave some reminiscences of the Queen's long and happy reign. There were large congregations at both services.[32] Three of the hymns sung during the day had been written and set to music by the Revd Williams. One hymn entitled 'Sixty years of Glorious Reign' contained the verse:

> *We pray that war and wrong may cease,*
> *That thou woulds't crown the world with peace,*
> *That Britain's flag may bear no stain*
> *To mar these years of glorious reign.*

There were two solos: Fred Gardner sang 'The Promise of the King', and his nephew, Master Sydney Cartmell, representing the Sunday school, sang 'The Chorister'. The Jubilee hymn 'O King of Kings' and the 'Te Deum' were heartily sung and a rousing rendition of 'God Save the Queen' closed both services.[33, 34]

On the Tuesday following, the actual anniversary of the Queen's accession, the festivities were said to have been the most successful in the town's history. A grand procession started from Market Place where 700 commemorative Diamond Jubilee medals were presented to the children. Following the procession people adjourned to the Royal Oak field where free refreshments were available and a programme of sports followed in the afternoon.[35]

Life at church continued much as usual. Roland Armstrong and his wife were appointed chapel keepers (caretakers). Their joint salary was £5 per annum plus an extra 10s. 0d. for additional tasks to be carried out once a year, or more often if necessary: washing all the painted woodwork, the pews, floors and both staircases, sweeping the ceiling, white washing the closet, blackening the grates, cleaning the window sills and umbrella stands, and checking the ventilation system.[36, 37] An extra ventilator had been placed in the organ loft and this exited at the top of the gable end of the chapel.

In order to reduce the debt of almost £160, which had arisen as a result of the alterations, it was decided to hold a bazaar. A newspaper report stated, 'the improvements have made this antiquated building more presentable'.[38]

A three day bazaar was held on November 10th, 11th and 13th 1897. A 40-page booklet was produced to advertise the bazaar and events taking place (Plate 12.6). It was prefaced by a brief history of the church and numerous local tradesmen took out full or half page adverts to help defray printing costs (Plates 12.4 and 12.5). At the top of many pages were quotes such as, 'We've all worked hard and done our best, may we appeal to you to do the rest?' and 'You are requested not to hurry before your money is done.' The bazaar was held in the Liberal Assembly Rooms. It was opened on the first day by F Thorp Esq JP of Ashton-on-Ribble and on the second by Robert Mansergh Esq. of Lancaster, secretary of the Preston district of the Lancashire Congregational Union.

At intervals throughout the three days there was entertainment given by 'an elocutionist, a humourist and numerous musicians', and a magic lantern show followed each evening. There was a 'Sunlight washing competition for

Plate 12.6 Pages from the Bazaar Booklet, 1897.

males only', during which young men were invited to prove their fitness, or otherwise, for matrimonial life by washing an article in a specified time. Young ladies were invited to watch the competition where they might learn something to their advantage.

For many months the ladies of the church had been holding sewing evenings in order to make articles for the bazaar. A report stated that the result of their efforts could be seen in the heavily laden stalls.[39] There was a wide variety of stalls: fancy, plain, toys, paper, furniture, crockery and refreshments. Mr S Pye, of Preston donated a wagon load of furniture and Mrs E Cartmell a sewing machine. The booklet stated, 'Closing time each evening 10 o'clock; but visitors who have emptied their purses may go earlier if they wish.' The bazaar closed on the third day with a jumble sale.

Edward Cartmell said that when the idea to hold a bazaar was first suggested he had no idea it would assume so large a scale. He heartily thanked everyone who had helped make the bazaar a success and said this included the many friends from other denominations in the neighbourhood. He said he was sure the Congregationalists in their turn would be willing to lend a hand when required. The grand total of £233 14s. 6d. was taken at the bazaar.[40] After expenses had been taken out and the debt on the chapel repaid, £40 13s. 6d. was handed to the treasurer. This money was put towards the purchase of land adjacent to the chapel for a new Sunday school building and caretaker's cottage.

Other fund raising events were held in the final years of the 19th century and in 1898 the land on the east side of the chapel was purchased from Major Bertram William Arnold Keppel, Lord of the Manor, for £75. The plot of land had a frontage of 48 feet and a depth of 107 feet.[41] The Sunday school building and caretaker's cottage were erected in the early years of the following century and were officially opened on June 29th 1904.

CHAPTER THIRTEEN

The Cartmell family

T HE NAME CARTMELL is woven through the tapestry of life at church for more than a hundred and seventy years. This chapter concentrates on those who played major roles in the church; those who made smaller contributions have been omitted.

John and Catherine Cartmell

The first Cartmells associated with the church were John and Catherine. John (1813–1902) was a son of William and Alice Cartmell of Goosnargh, and Catherine a daughter of Edward Seed, farmer, of St Michaels-on-Wyre. They were married on August 27th 1838 at St Helens, Churchtown, and made their home at Barnacre with Bonds.[1, 2] John, a tailor by trade, was also a grocer and sub-postmaster for about 45 years prior to his death (Plate 13.1).[3] Following John's death Miss Mary J Trippear who had been his housekeeper and shop assistant took over as postmistress.[4] She had lived with the Cartmell's since being a teenager and was also a member of the church.

John and Catherine had at least fourteen children, seven of whom died young and were interred at Churchtown.[5] Four of their sons: Edward, John, Robert and Moses, were to play prominent roles in the life of Garstang Congregational Church, Edward probably having the greatest influence. Catherine died in 1882 aged 65 and John in 1902 aged 88. His obituary describes him as the oldest resident in the district. The hearse was followed

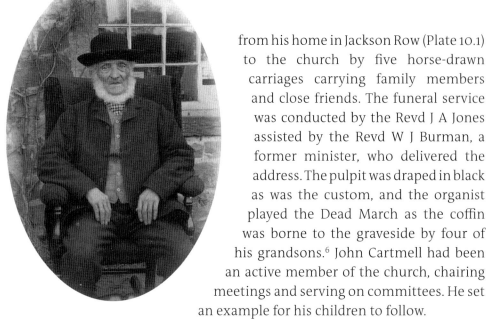

from his home in Jackson Row (Plate 10.1) to the church by five horse-drawn carriages carrying family members and close friends. The funeral service was conducted by the Revd J A Jones assisted by the Revd W J Burman, a former minister, who delivered the address. The pulpit was draped in black as was the custom, and the organist played the Dead March as the coffin was borne to the graveside by four of his grandsons.[6] John Cartmell had been an active member of the church, chairing meetings and serving on committees. He set an example for his children to follow.

Edward, John, Robert and Moses, sons of John and Catherine Cartmell

Edward (1842–1907) the eldest of the four brothers began attending Sunday school when he was five years old; this was the start of his life-long service to the church.[7] He later became a teacher and Sunday school superintendent. At 23 he became a seat holder, i.e. paid rent for his own seat in church.[8] In 1868 he took over from Dr Bell as church secretary, a post he was to hold for 39 years. He also served as church treasurer, deacon and delegate representing the church at Lancashire Congregational Union meetings. A life-long teetotaller he did much to advance the cause of temperance in Garstang through the Congregational Band of Hope and Temperance Society. He served on several committees involving the fabric of the church and together with his brother, John, was one of the prime movers in the establishment of the Sunday school building. Thorough in his work he made frequent notes, recorded every tiny expense and was meticulous in his record keeping. Many of his note books have survived and it is thanks to him that so much information about the church in the late 19th century is known.

In 1868 Edward married Agnes Brockbank Blacklock at Lancaster High Street Independent Chapel.[9] There were ten children of the marriage (Plate 13.3). One died in infancy and over the years four emigrated to the United

Plate 13.2 Advert for Edward Cartmell's Shops, 1897.

States of America. He started his business as a tailor and draper in the High Street, shortly afterwards acquiring a larger premises in Market Place and some years later purchasing a third shop in Fleetwood (Plate 13.2).[10]

Edward was a founder member of Garstang Liberal Club and served for a time as president. A prominent member of the Oddfellows he had at various times held all the offices in connection with the District and Loyal Adelaide Lodge. He was a member of the Parish council from its inception and a manager of Garstang Grammar School.

He suffered from diabetes, a condition which affected several members of the Cartmell family.[11] In March 1907 he developed a virulent form of carbuncle and it was deemed necessary to operate. Unfortunately complications ensued and he died on Good Friday, March 29th. He was 64 years old.

On the day of his funeral the whole town went into mourning for one of its most respected citizens. All businesses closed and blinds were drawn. His coffin was borne by members of the Loyal Adelaide Lodge from his home in Market Place to the Congregational Church. The choir gallery was draped in black, and white flowers adorned the pulpit. As the church was without

Plate 13.3 Edward and Agnes Cartmell and their children.

a minister the Revd J A Jones, the previous minister, took the service. Local newspapers reported:

> Mr Cartmell was a man of genial and charitable disposition, and unimpeachable character and, by the exercise of strict integrity had built up a successful business. His loss would be felt not only by his wife, six sons and three daughters, and his wide circle of friends, but also by the town and the Congregational denomination as a whole.[12, 13]

Two of his daughters, Ethel and May, gave two metal trays to hold communion glasses, in memory of their parents, Edward and Agnes. These trays are still in use today.

It is fitting that shortly after his death a memorial tablet was erected on the opposite side of the pulpit to that of Dr Bell. These two Christian men had between them served the church as secretary for almost 80 years.

John Cartmell (1846–1927) married Elizabeth (Lizzie) Swarbrick of Wardleys and they had a tailor and drapers shop in Market Place (Plates 13.4 and 13.5).[14, 15] After Lizzie died he married Catherine Gunn. There were no children of either marriage. For more than 60 years he was associated with the Oddfellows and the Loyal Adelaide Lodge. He was a founder member of Garstang Liberal Club, a director of Garstang Gas Company, and a trustee of Baylton's Charity. A progressive educationalist, he carried out his duties as a manager of Garstang Grammar School with great diligence. His obituary described him as a man of integrity and unfailing courtesy.[16]

Plate 13.4 John Cartmell Jnr

He and his brother, Edward, supported each other's church projects. In the mid-1890s he was one of the people responsible for having an organ loft and singing gallery erected at the front of the church. Being a generous man, he made frequent gifts to the church. He was one of the prime movers in the building of the Sunday school, was treasurer of the building fund to which he donated 50 guineas, and was overseer of the building work. When he retired his drapery business was taken over by Richard Storey, his employee, who had married his niece, Lizzie Swarbrick.[17, 18]

Robert Cartmell (1853–1897), married Jane Gardner daughter of Robert Gardner, a deacon of the church.[19] They had two sons, Allan and Sidney Herbert Cromwell Cartmell. Allan died in infancy.[20] Robert served on several committees with respect to the fabric of the church. He was secretary of the Band of Hope and Temperance Society for many years. Both he and his son were talented musicians. For 17 years Robert played the harmonium in church and was also the choir leader. In 1893 when a more modern organ was purchased his nephew, William Harold Cartmell took his place.[21] He was a member of the Garstang and District Liberal Association, the Independent Order of Oddfellows and the Loyal Adelaide Lodge. Robert followed the family tradition becoming a tailor and had a shop in the High Street. He might well have had an advert in the bazaar booklet of November 1897 had it not been for his sudden death of typhoid fever one month before the event, at the age of 44 years.[22]

Plate 13.5 John Cartmell's Tailor and Draper's Shop on right and Royal Oak on left. Card posted 1908.

Moses Cartmell (1858–1917) the youngest of the four brothers, married Margaret Whittaker, a dressmaker from Barton near Preston.[23, 24] Their only child, Maud, died in infancy.[25] Initially he followed in the family footsteps becoming a draper's assistant. He was a Liberal in politics and, following the opening of the Liberal club in Bridge Street, became its caretaker/steward.[26] He then became a pork butcher and for the next 20 years rented a shop in Stoops Hall Buildings on the High Street, later to become part of W H Singleton, pork butchers (Plate 13.6).[27]

He was on the building committee whilst the Sunday school was being erected and subsequently on the management committee. He was authorised to witness marriages in church and, in 1911, was treasurer of the new organ fund. He and his wife donated three dozen chairs to the Sunday school, and book prizes for Sunday school attendance, in 1907, the first year they were awarded.[28] At

Plate 13.6 Advert for Moses Cartmell, Pork Butcher, Stoops Hall Buildings, 1897.

M. Cartmell,

Pork & Provision Dealer,

Stoops Hall Buildings,
GARSTANG.

Home-cured Hams and Bacon.—Finest Quality.

Home-rendered Lard.

Pork Pies, Sausages and Black Puddings, own make, stand unequalled for flavour and unvarying quality.

LARGE PIES MADE TO ORDER.

A trial respectfully solicited.

the time of his death he was living at Ashfield, Nateby (formerly the church manse), was chairman of Garstang Parish Council, a member of the Town Trust, a director of Garstang Gas Company, and a manager of Garstang Grammar School.[29]

William Harold and Herbert, two sons of Edward Cartmell

William Harold Cartmell (1873–1957) was the second son of Edward Cartmell. On the death of his father, Harold and his brother Ernest took over the family drapery business at Fleetwood. Harold had been the organist at Garstang for a number of years, following his uncle Robert in 1893. Harold married Dorothy Riley, the daughter of a prominent Fleetwood builder. Whilst living in Fleetwood he became organist and secretary of Fleetwood Congregational Church. On moving back to Garstang in 1923 he resumed his membership of Garstang Congregational Church and became treasurer, secretary, and organist once again. He built Lowood, a bungalow on Croston Road, the first domestic dwelling in Garstang to be equipped with electricity. It had a specially built engine room containing a generator at the bottom of their garden.[30] He was a member of Garstang Rural District council 1927–1952 and chairman 1938–1939. He was a trustee of Baylton's Charity and a former chairman of the Finance Committee of Garstang Town Trust.[31]

Following the death of his wife he married again. His second wife was Dorothy Kirby. There were no children of either marriage. During the years 1919–1934 the church was without a resident minister. The Revd William Shakespeare Rowland of Elswick had pastoral oversight of the church and Harold, being secretary, was in charge of pulpit supplies. He grew tired of organising preachers every week and in 1934, purchased Number 2 Beechmount, Garstang (Plate 11.1), a substantial semi-detached house next to the railway bridge, for the use of the church as a manse, in the hope of attracting a resident minister.[32, 33] Later that year the Revd Thomas (Tommy) Ormerod, a former physics master at Manchester Grammar School, became the church's minister.[34] In 1946, Harold made a gift of the manse to the church.[35] The church sold the manse in 1965 and purchased another on Lancaster Road.

Whilst Harold was treasurer and organist the church purchased an Ainscough pipe organ from the Harris Orphanage in Garstang Road, Preston (Plate 13.7).[36] Tommy Railton, was the first organ blower, followed by Harold's nephews, Edward (Ted) and Ben, who shared organ blowing duties. The Revd Tommy Ormerod, having a physics background, constructed an electric blower – a somewhat Heath-Robinson affair, and the boys were made redundant.[37] Harold retired from the position of organist in 1948 after 25 years continuous service, making 39 years in total at Garstang. (He had also been organist at Fleetwood for several years.) During the church restoration of 1984, the organ was found to be riddled with woodworm and the cost of repair prohibitive, so it was scrapped and replaced by an electronic one.

Herbert Cartmell (1880–1962) was Edward Cartmell's fourth son. In 1909 he married Agnes Ethel Lancaster, daughter of James Lancaster, station-master of Garstang and Catterall railway station. In their early childhood both Herbert and Agnes Ethel attended a dames' school in the house of Miss James. This was opposite St Thomas's Church and next door to where Dr Bell had once lived. Agnes Ethel was a staunch Anglican and they were married at St Thomas's Church by the Revd Boys Stones. They had five children but only four lived to adulthood: Katherine, Dorothy, Edward (Ted) and Benjamin.[38]

On his father's death Herbert took over the Garstang business in Market Place, Garstang. When he retired he moved into 1 Beechmount, Garstang, next door to the property given to the church by his brother.

He was a member of the Town Trust for 40 years, chairman of the Liberal club committee for 40 years and deacon of the church for 50.[39]

He was a staunch Congregationalist and their children were brought up as Congregationalists. On his father's death, he took over as Sunday school superintendent. Two years later he became church secretary. He had a fine voice and, together with his cousin Sidney and two friends, formed a quartet which was in great demand at church concerts and elsewhere. He was a member of the church choir from being a young man until his death. When he died, he left the church a small legacy which was invested in Garstang Rural District Council at 5.5%.[40]

Katherine, Dorothy, Edward (Ted) and Benjamin, children of Herbert Cartmell

Katherine (Kath) (1910–1985) taught at Nateby County Primary School for 35 years. A keen historian she was eager to preserve the old buildings of Garstang and was made an honorary life member of the town's Heritage society. She was a member of Garstang Town Trust for many years, and served as committee member and secretary of the town's Women's Institute.

She was a founder member of Garstang Choral Society and a member of the church choir. Devoted to her church she served as member, deacon,

Plate 13.7 Interior of Chapel, 1927, showing Ainscough Pipe Organ. Photo: Preston Guardian 21 May 1927.

elder, secretary and Sunday school teacher. On her father's death, she became Sunday school superintendent, following her father Herbert, and grandfather Edward in an unbroken sequence of 100 years.[41,42]

Dorothy (1913–1973) was a Sunday school scholar, teacher and member of the choir for many years. In her youth she was a member of a team which won the Pemberton Shield. This was awarded by the Lancashire Congregational Union to the church whose children gained most marks in a religious knowledge examination. Garstang Church won the shield six times between 1929 and 1944. The shield was first awarded in 1920 and Garstang was the first country church to win it.[43] In 1931 Dorothy passed the intermediate examination with honours and was awarded a special prize by the Preston district of the Lancashire Congregational Union.[44]

Dorothy served in the ATS during World War II. She married William Green from Salford, a haberdashery representative. They had three children: Janet, Alan and Robert, and it is through their children and grandchildren the long association with the church continues. When her father retired in 1952, they took over the business in Market Place, and later the Fleetwood one as well. Although the business name changed to 'Greens', people in Garstang still referred to it as Cartmells. The shop closed in 1971, having been associated with the Cartmell family for 98 years.[45]

Edward (Ted) (1916–2003) attended Lancaster Royal Grammar School. He was a member of the Sunday school and for several years was part of a group of children awarded the Pemberton shield for religious knowledge. In 1931 he was awarded a special prize for gaining the highest mark in an All England religious examination organised by the Congregational churches.[46] During part of the time his uncle was organist he and his brother Ben took it in turns to be organ blowers. Ted was also the magic lantern operator at some of the entertainments. On leaving school he went to University College, London, to study chemistry. On graduation he began research in the field of Raman spectroscopy. The outbreak of war saw him evacuated, first to Wales and then Southampton. He joined the RAF in 1942 then, after cessation of hostilities, joined the chemistry department at University College, Southampton (later Southampton University), where he was to stay for the next 30 years. He was a keen musician and capable organist, playing the pipe organ in Garstang Congregational Church whenever he came north to visit his family. He was a chorister at Avenue Saint Andrew's Church, Southampton, for 51 years and choirmaster for 22.[47] When he died in 2003 he left a generous legacy to Garstang United Reformed Church which went towards the refurbishment of the church hall.[48]

Benjamin (Ben) (1920–1943) like his brother, went to Lancaster Royal Grammar School. He was keen on all aspects of radio. He attended a college in Preston which trained radio operators for the merchant navy. The outbreak of World War II saw him as second radio officer sailing in ships owned by a Liverpool shipping line. He served in the Merchant Navy, 1939–1943, and was lost at sea by enemy action off Freetown, West Africa on April 30th 1943. His parents, Herbert and Ethel, gave the stained glass window on the west wall of the church in his memory. The window shows the insignia of the Merchant Navy and the lightning flashes of a radio operator.[49]

The window opposite, on the east wall, was presented to the church in 1984 by the then surviving grandchildren of Edward Cartmell (1842–1907), i.e. Kath and Edward (Ted) Cartmell, and Jack and Ted Cutler. (Edward Cartmell's daughter, Ethel, had married Lawrence Cutler of Nateby and they had emigrated to Iowa, USA.) The window was given to commemorate links the family had with the church over many years, and as a contribution to the 1984 refurbishment. The window shows symbols of the Christian faith: the cross, the chalice and the open Bible. Both windows were designed and made by Abbott and Co. of Lancaster.[50,51] It is fitting that there is a memorial window commemorating the Cartmell family and the faithful service they gave to the church over several generations.

• CHAPTER FOURTEEN •

Miscellanea

T HIS CLOSING CHAPTER is reserved for a few facts that could not easily be woven into the history of the church, but which are, nevertheless, too interesting to be omitted.

The Walpole–Keppel Connection

Sir Edward Walpole KB (1706–1784) purchased the Manor of Garstang from the Crown in 1750.[1] He was the second son of Sir Robert Walpole and brother of Horatio (Horace) Walpole, the author. Sir Edward followed his father into politics and held many high ranking positions.

When in his twenties Edward went on the Grand Tour of Europe and on his return, in 1830, he began frequenting Mrs Rennie's milliner's shop, near London's Pall Mall. There he fell in love with one of the apprentices, Dorothy Mary Clement, daughter of Hammond Clement, a postmaster from County Durham. Mrs Rennie, seeing the blossoming romance and fearing the disgrace of her employee, summoned Dorothy's father to her shop. Mr Clement and Mrs Rennie persuaded Dorothy that she ought to return to County Durham with her father. Dorothy agreed to go, but had no intention of doing so. She said she would go and pack her belongings but, instead of packing, she ran out of the back of the shop and across to Edward's house in Pall Mall. There she poured her heart out to him. He had no intention of losing the love of his life, so he took her in and sat her down at the head of his table, a position she held for the rest of her life. In order not to incur the wrath of his father Edward did not marry Dorothy; she had no title or dowry, and was of lowly origin. Instead, they lived together and Dorothy bore him three daughters, Laura, Maria and Charlotte, and a son, Edward. Unfortunately Dorothy died soon after the birth of their son. The children were brought up as Walpoles, not Clements. Sir Edward never married, but devoted his life to the children's upbringing. Edward junior entered the army and died unmarried in his early thirties. Despite the drawback of their illegitimacy the girls made advantageous marriages. The eldest, Laura, married The Honourable Revd Frederick Keppel, the future Bishop of Exeter and Dean of Windsor. He was the youngest son of the 2nd Earl of Albemarle and a great grandson of King Charles II. (The 2nd Earl of Albemarle married Lady Anne Lennox, daughter of Charles Lennox, Duke of Richmond, an illegitimate son of King Charles II by his French mistress Louise de Kéroualle.) The Keppel family seat was Lexham Hall, Norfolk.[2, 3, 4, 5]

Horace Walpole, the writer, was devoted to his nieces. His friend, James, 2nd Earl of Waldegrave, was Lord of the Treasury in His Majesty King George II's government. James was not only a minister, but also the King's adviser and confidante. Horace introduced James, a bachelor aged 43, to Maria aged 22, and they were married soon afterwards. It was a happy marriage despite the difference in age. Maria bore him three daughters, but unfortunately after five years she was widowed; James died of smallpox. After a suitable period of mourning Maria married His Royal Highness, Prince William Henry, Duke of Gloucester, a brother of King George III. This marriage enraged the King as his brother had married an illegitimate commoner and was, with the subsequent marriage of another of his brothers, the Duke of Cumberland, to another commoner, the cause of the passing of the Royal Marriage Act 1772. This Act required all descendants of King George II to seek the Sovereign's approval before marriage.

Maria died in 1807 and was buried with her husband, the Duke of Gloucester, in St George's Chapel, Windsor. Laura, too, was buried with her husband, Bishop Keppel, in the same chapel. And so two illegitimate daughters of a milliner's assistant were buried amidst royalty; Queen Elizabeth, the Queen Mother, joining them in 2002.

Sir Edward's youngest daughter, Charlotte, married Lord Huntingtower, heir to the Dysart fortune. There were no children of this marriage.

When Sir Edward died, his daughter Laura was already a widow; Bishop Keppel having died in 1777 (the year Garstang Independent Chapel was founded). Sir Edward died a wealthy man and left a very detailed will. His house at Isleworth, Middlesex, was left to Laura outright. He left several manors: Garstang in Lancashire, Newbiggin in Westmoreland, and several in the south of England. He entailed his Manor of Garstang as far as his great grandsons. This meant his descendants could draw the rents and enjoy the privileges that went with the estate, but they were not free to sell. This was to ensure that, as far as possible, the estate remained in the family. The first person to hold it was his daughter, Laura.[6] (Perhaps he was concerned that if Laura were to re-marry, his estate would pass out of the family.) He was generous with his family, his friends, his servants, and also with the Clement family. He left annuities to Dorothy's mother, sister and aunt. One of the Clement legacies was an annuity of £400.

On Laura's death in 1813 the estate passed to her son, Frederick Keppel junior, who had three sons: Frederick Walpole Keppel, Colonel Edward George Walpole Keppel and the Revd William Arnold Walpole Keppel. (Most Keppel men, other than the eldest in the family, were either in the armed forces or men of the cloth.)

In order to understand why the Revd Keppel put Garstang up for sale in 1867 (Chapter 6), it is necessary to go back to the will of his father, Frederick Keppel, junior, which stated that his estates should pass to his three sons, 'successively according to seniority'.[7] His eldest son, Frederick Walpole Keppel, had two daughters, Fanny and Louisa, but no sons. His second son, Colonel Keppel, died unmarried and without issue. His youngest son, the Revd Keppel had three sons and a daughter.

The eldest of the three brothers died when his daughters, Fanny and Louisa, were minors, aged eight and nine. In order to provide for them it was a condition of his will that they should each inherit £15,000 on reaching their majority of 21 years, or on marriage, if younger, provided it was with the consent of their guardians.[8] The estates then passed to Colonel Keppel, who survived his brother by only eleven months, and then to the Revd Keppel, rector of Haynford, Norfolk. As time drew near for the girls to receive their inheritance it was necessary for the Revd Keppel to raise the capital. As Garstang had been entailed by Sir Edward Walpole only as far as his great-grandsons, the Revd Keppel was free to sell. Garstang was put up for auction in 1867. The highest bid, £78,000, was below the reserve price, so the town was withdrawn from sale. However, over the following years some properties were sold privately. A release document of 1875 states that both Fanny and Louisa had received their inheritance, the Revd Keppel having raised the money by sale of part of the Garstang estate and by mortgaging other parts.[9]

It was not until 1919 that the remaining properties owned by the Keppels were sold either privately or at auction.[10] Thus an era spanning almost 170 years, when the town was owned by this family, came to an end.

In the late 1930s the name Kettle Lane was changed to Kepple Lane to reflect the history of the town; unfortunately the spelling is not quite that of the previous owners.[11]

The Keppels are still remembered in Garstang. On festive occasions a banner displaying their coat of arms is hung in the High Street together with the arms of other notable local families. The Keppel arms is described: Gules, three escallops argent, i.e. three silver scallop shells on a red background. The scallop shells are the sign of a Christian pilgrimage; their motto 'ne cede malis' means 'yield not to misfortunes'.[12]

Robert Doggett (1819–1899)

Robert Doggett and his wife Pamela were born at Hethersett in Norfolk.[13] A military man, he served as a colour sergeant in HM Coldstream Guards. He was one of the bearers at the funeral of Field Marshall, HRH the Duke of Cambridge, the youngest son of King George III. Following the funeral, which took place at Kew on July 16th 1850, Robert Doggett was presented with a commemorative medal by the Duke's family.[14] When he retired he and his wife moved to Barnacre-with-Bonds to be near their daughter, Catherine, who had married Edwin Curwen.[15] The Curwens attended the Congregational Church and Robert Doggett became a member in 1893. He died on September 22nd 1899 and was interred in the grounds of Garstang Congregational Church. His name and that of his wife are engraved on the tombstone of his daughter and son-in-law, but graveyard records show they are not buried there. They are buried in a nearby grave marked by a small stone, eight inches high, on which is inscribed R and P Doggett.

Edward Dawson, Edward Bousfield Dawson and Robert Mansergh

These three Lancaster men were staunch Congregationalists, members of High Street Chapel, Lancaster, and supporters of the Lancashire Congregational Union. The church at Garstang had its ups and downs regarding finance and ministers, and sometimes seemed uncooperative with the Congregational Union. However, whatever the situation and whatever the official ruling of the Union, these men never wavered in their support for the church at Garstang and were generous benefactors of its many causes (Plates 14.1, 14.2 and 14.3).[16, 17, 18]

The Dawson family had been staunch supporters of Independency and Congregationalism over many generations. Mrs Isabel Dawson, widow of Robert Dawson, of Aldcliffe Hall, Lancaster, and grandmother of Edward Dawson, worshipped at Forton Independent Chapel accompanied by her faithful dog, in the years before High Street Chapel, Lancaster, was erected. Her grandfather was responsible for the building of the Independent Chapel at Newton in Bowland in 1696.[19] In Forton United Reformed Church there is a large carved wooden memorial in her memory.

Plate 14.1 Edward Dawson 1793–1876

Edward Dawson JP (1793–1876), of Aldcliffe Hall, Lancaster, and his son Edward Bousfield Dawson LLB JP (1830–1916) served the Preston district of the Lancashire Congregational Union for many years. Between them they served as secretary for eleven years and treasurer for sixty.[20] At the time of his death Edward Bousfield Dawson was chairman of the Lancaster Quarter Sessions, chairman of Lancaster Rural District Council, chairman of the Lancaster Board of Guardians, president of Lancaster Total Abstinence Society, president of the Lancashire Farmers' Association (he was one of the largest landowners in the district), Constable of Lancaster Castle and chairman or president of many other organisations. His portrait hangs in Lancaster Castle.

Following his funeral service at the Centenary Congregational Chapel, Lancaster, his remains were interred in the private burial ground at his home, Aldcliffe Hall.[21]

As this family had supported the church at Garstang over many years, it was appropriate that when the new Sunday school building was opened, on June 29th 1904, Edward Bousfield Dawson should be invited to perform the opening ceremony.[22]

Plate 14.2 Edward Bousfield Dawson 1830–1916

Plate 14.3 Robert Mansergh 1833–1914

Robert Mansergh JP (1833–1914), a Lancaster business man, had a draper's shop in Market Square. He was a local preacher, chairman of the Lancashire Congregational Union in 1894, secretary of the Preston district for 32 years, treasurer of the Congregational Total Abstinence Society, and held many influential positions in public life.[23] When the church at Garstang was without a minister, he frequently chaired its meetings. He was invited to be the opener on the second day of a three-day bazaar held in 1897 (Chapter 12), and in his opening speech said that a church was not a building or an edifice, it was a community of Christian people, pledged to do good work for Christ. He went on to say that the church at Garstang had remained steadfast to the Nonconformist cause.[24]

Lizzie Swarbrick

(Lizzie was the artist who painted the flowers and the vine on the panels fronting the organ loft.)

Elizabeth, known as Lizzie, was born in 1874 at Wardley's Ferry, Staynall, on the river Wyre. Both her father and grandfather were ferrymen.[25] When 10 years old she went to live with her father's sister, Lizzie, wife of John Cartmell of Garstang. Her aunt and uncle had a draper's shop in the town and she became a draper's assistant.[26] Lizzie's name first appeared on the Sunday school register in October 1885, and in 1891 she became a Sunday school teacher. In 1885 she joined the Band of Hope and Temperance Society.[27] John and Lizzie Cartmell had no children, but treated Lizzie as if she were their own. The late Ted Cartmell, grandson of

Plate 14.4 Lizzie Swarbrick (Mrs Richard Storey)

Edward Cartmell (Chapter 13), described her as being 'sort of adopted by the Cartmells'. According to Ted, Lizzie showed promise as an artist, so her uncle, John Cartmell, paid for her to have tuition in painting.[28]

In the mid-1890s it was decided to build an organ loft and singing gallery at the front of the church as several organs had been ruined by dampness on the ground floor. John Cartmell was one of the prime movers in this decision and the work was completed in 1897. The church minutes of June 1st 1897 record 'Miss Swarbrick's offer to decorate the panels in front of the singing gallery be accepted with thanks'. She was 23 years old (Plate 14.4). The vine and flower paintings show exceptional talent and are a most unusual feature in the church (Plate 14.5). In the 1890s the interior of the church was highly decorated and colourful compared with the decoration today. The paintings could possibly have been Lizzie's way of thanking her uncle for his kindness to her.

In 1902 she married Richard Storey in the church, and looking down on them were the flower paintings she had painted five years earlier. In 1984 the church underwent a thorough renovation and restoration and, as part of the work, the paintings were cleaned and restored. Lizzie and Richard had three children, Ellen (Nellie), Betty and Stanley, all of whom attended Sunday school.

Plate 14.5 Panels showing the Vine and Flower Paintings

Frederick (Fred) Gardner (1877–1920)

Fred came from a family of boot and shoe makers, whose business in Bridge Street, Garstang, had been established in 1810.[29] He was the youngest child of Robert and Elizabeth Gardner, born when they were in their late 40s.[30] On leaving school he worked in the family business. Fred was 14 when his father died, and this was followed by his mother's death 3 years later. His sister, Jane, married Robert Cartmell, a brother of Edward Cartmell, and they had a son, Sidney Herbert Cromwell Cartmell, six years after Fred was born.[31, 32] Sidney was 13 when his father died.[33] The 1901 census shows Sidney H C Cartmell, a tailor's apprentice aged 17, living with his uncle Fred Gardner, a boot maker aged 23, of Bridge street, Garstang (Plate 14.6). The two young men had fine voices and were in great demand both at church and other places locally (Plate 14.7).

Fred's father, Robert, had been a staunch supporter of the church, serving as deacon, treasurer of the Band of Hope and Temperance Society, trustee of the first manse, as well as holding other offices. Fred was also a staunch supporter of the church, following in many of his father's footsteps. He became a Sunday school scholar and teacher. He joined the Band of Hope and Temperance society taking the pledge in 1900 never to drink intoxicating liquor.[34] He served on the church management committee, the committee for the building of the new Sunday school, and became church treasurer in 1907 for a short time following the death of Edward Cartmell.[35] In 1901 he married Ellen Thomas, daughter of Garstang chemist, Jonathan Jowett Thomas, a member of the church. (There were many marriages between

Plate 14.6 Fred Gardner in his Shop on Bridge Street

Plate 14.7 Band
of Hope and
Temperance
Society
Concert, 1899

CONGREGATIONAL
Band of Hope and Temperance Society.
GARSTANG.

The Anniversary Meeting
Will be held in the Assembly Rooms,

ON TUESDAY EVENING, APRIL 18th, 1899.

TO COMMENCE AT 7-30.

THE REV. J. A. JONES IN THE CHAIR.

PROGRAMME.

1	Chairman's Address.		
2	Song	"The Holy City."	MR. F. GARDNER
3	Recitation		MISS MASON, of Barton
4	Address	G. MASON, Esq., President of the Preston and District Band of Hope Union	
5	Duet	"The Moon hath raised her lamp above."	MESSRS. F. GARDNER & R. BOND
6	Recitation	..."Llewellyn and his Dog."	MASTER HARRY THOMAS
7	Recitation	..."Cheer, Boys, Cheer!"	MASTER TED CARTMELL
8	Recitation	"Adam and Mary."	MASTER SYDNEY CARTMELL
9	Song		MISS CURWEN
10	Recitation		MISS MASON
11	Address		MR. CHRIS. McNEAL
12	Song	"The heart bow'd down."	MR. F. GARDNER
		Doxology.	

Collection will be taken to assist in defraying expenses.
ALL ARE INVITED.

H. Wrightson, Printer, Post Office, Garstang.

families at the church.) The church management committee presented Fred with a case of silver spoons on the occasion of his marriage, 'in recognition of the services he had rendered to the church'.[36] Fred and Ellen had three children: Robert born 1907, Jane 1909 and Edward 1911.

Sometime before December 1915 Fred and his family moved to St Helens where he continued with his occupation as a boot and shoe maker. Fred saw action in World War I. In December 1915 he enlisted as a reservist in the 3rd South Lancashire Regiment. His army records state he was 5 foot 6 inches tall, just under 10 stone in weight, medically A1 and of good

Plate 14.8 Stone carving, by the High Street

character. His regiment embarked for France on June 27th 1917 and he was posted to the 8th Battalion. On arrival in Rouen he was transferred to the 2nd/6th Battalion of the Royal Warwickshire Regiment and joined his unit on the battlefield.[37] His battalion was deployed in the following battles: Langemark (August 1917); Cambrai (December 1917); St Quentin (March 1918); the Somme Crossing (March 1918) and the Lys (April 1918).[38] On the 11th November 1918 when the Armistice was signed his battalion was south of Valenciennes. He was demobilised on February 20th 1919 with a certificate stating that he was not suffering from any disability caused by his military service.[39] He was awarded the British War Medal (silver), awarded to those who served overseas, and the Victory Medal (bronze), awarded to those who saw action in a theatre of war.

After the war he continued with his occupation as a boot and shoe maker at St Helens. He died of a perforated ulcer on February 8th 1920, fifteen months after the armistice, and was buried at Garstang Congregational Church in the northern part of the graveyard. Ellen, his wife, died in 1953 aged 81 years. Correspondence exists between the church and the war graves' commission stating his grave should be recognised as a war grave.[40]

In February 1944 Fred's son and wife, Robert and Elizabeth, who lived at Castle View, Bonds, Garstang, had their daughter, Elizabeth Ann, baptised at the church. A note in the church records states that the grandparents of Elizabeth Ann were formerly members of the church. This is the last record of this family having connections with the church.

John and Henry Sawyer

In 1851 the name John Sawyer was carved on a stone wall by the High Street (Plate 14.8). Who was this man? Census records show only one John Sawyer, stonemason, living in the area. He lived with his wife Lucy and children at Hill Beck, Barnacre (now Bees Hill).[41] John and Lucy Sawyer, of Barnacre-with-Bonds, had their children: Mary, Henry, Lucy and Betty, baptised at the Independent Chapel, Garstang. Henry became a stonemason like his father. A wages book, beginning in 1855, exists for people employed part-time on the Keppel estate.[42] Henry was a valued employee; in 1867 he was paid a daily wage of 4s. 6d. but other workmen were paid only 2s. 6d. He was employed to repair walls in the town and to put stone flags down in the street. It took him six days to flag the Royal Oak kitchen floor. In 1873 Henry built the stone walls to the north and west of the Independent Chapel to enclose the extended graveyard; these walls still exist today.

Plate 14.9 One of the Tapestries stitched in 1986

Ebenezer Le Mare (Chapter 10)

The Le Mare family can trace its roots back to the Huguenots (French protestants persecuted by Catholic France). The family arrived in England in the late 1600s with little more than their religious faith and a determination to make an honest living. They were skilled silk workers and were active in the silk industry for about 200 years. Ebenezer was intensely proud of his Huguenot ancestry and named one of his sons, Harold Huguenot Le Mare. It is probably Ebenezer's youngest son, Noël Hamer Le Mare, who is best remembered today. He was the owner of the racehorse, Red Rum, which won The Grand National three times.[43]

People with Church connections going back four generations

Mildred Kelsall, a member of the congregation, is a great granddaughter of James Clark, who served the church as deacon, chairman of meetings and auditor of church accounts (Chapters 7 and 9).

Colin Armstrong, an elder of the church, and his sister, Hazel Atkinson (née Armstrong), a church member, are the fourth generation of their family to be associated with the church. Their great grandparents, William and Mary, are buried in the grave next but one to Dr Bell. William was an innkeeper of the Swan Inn, Garstang. When the Swan Inn was demolished it was replaced by the Crown Hotel which was built to the north of the Swan Inn and further back from the road. In a grave a little further on are their grandparents, Roland and Elizabeth. At the end of the 19th century Roland and Elizabeth were chapel keepers (caretakers). Colin and Hazel's parents, Thomas and Annie, are buried in the newer part of the graveyard between the church and Sunday school. Annie was a deacon of the church and helped stitch the tapestries, designed by Anne Stanley, which are an interesting feature in the church (Plate 14.9). (Other ladies who worked on the tapestries, in 1986, were: Ella Abbott, Alice Crook, Lucy Crone, Edith Entwistle, Anne Humphreys, Eileen Jackson, Elizabeth Lund, Bessie Stephenson and Ann Wicks.)

...And what of the future?

This book covers only the first part of the church's history. As we move into the 21st century Christians continue to meet regularly for worship at this little church and the precious faith which our Nonconformist forefathers established in Garstang over two centuries ago continues to hold firm.

• MINISTERS OF THE CHURCH •

1777	Church founded, possibly as a joint pastorate with Forton, or under the pastoral care of Abram Allot [sic] minister of Forton
1784 – 1787	George Richardson
1788 – 1791	Under the pastoral care of Timothy Senior, minister of Elswick, and Abraham Allert, minister of Forton
1792 – 1794	Under the pastoral care of Timothy Senior minister of Elswick, and James Grimshaw, minister of Forton
1794 – 1828	Joint pastorate of Garstang and Forton with James Grimshaw, minister

The following ministers were appointed to the Garstang pastorate only:

1829 – 1835	Edward Edwards
1839 – 1846	William Craig
1847 – 1854	John Spencer
1854 – 1875	Interregnum. Under the pastoral care of visiting ministers and lay preachers
1875 – 1879	John Schofield
1880 – 1882	Joseph Cockram
1888 – 1891	William Jeffcoat Burman
1891 – 1896	John James Williams
1897 – 1906	John Angell Jones B A
1907 – 1909	Benjamin Hargreaves
1911 – 1914	Harry Ingham M A
1915 – 1917	J B Parry
1919 – 1934	Interregnum. Under the pastoral care of William Shakespeare Rowland of Elswick
1934 – 1938	Thomas Ormerod B Sc

The following ministers were appointed to the joint pastorate of Garstang and Forton:

1938 – 1945	Thomas Ormerod B Sc
1945 – 1951	Richard Thompson
1952 – 1958	Norman Burgoine
1960 – 1965	Derek Haley B D
1966 – 1971	George Arthur Abbott
1972 – 1981	Margaret W Taylor
1981 – 1985	Albert Greasley
1987 – 1989	Alan Cole
1990 – 1994	Joan Grindrod
1995 – 2000	Barry Hutchinson B Th
2002 – 2009	David Greenwood

• REFERENCES •

Abbreviations

Ibid.	Reference is the same as the previous one.
op. cit.	Reference used previously in this chapter.
LRO Ref.	Lancashire Record Office reference number.
CR.	Church records (still in possession of the church).
Passim.	Several parts of the book referred to.

Chapter One

1. *The New World Library Encyclopaedia*, The Caxton Publishing Co Ltd, 1965.
2. Halley Robert, *Lancashire: Its Puritanism and Nonconformity*, Tubbs & Brook, 11 Market Street, Manchester, 1872, p 50.
3. Jones R Tudur, *Congregationalism in England, 1662–1962*, The Independent Press Ltd., Memorial Hall, London, EC4, pp 17–18.
4. Robinson W. Gordon, MA, BD, PhD., *A History of the Lancashire Congregational Union 1806–1956*, Lancashire Congregational Union, 244 Deansgate, Manchester 3, p 16.
5. Ibid, p 18.
6. Bennet T, *Laws against Nonconformity*, Roberts & Jackson, 4 Victoria Street, Grimsby, 1913, pp 125–134.
7. Nightingale B, *Centenary of the Lancashire Congregational Union 1806–1906*, John Heywood Ltd. Manchester, p 74.
8. Hone William, *The Everyday Book*, Hunt and Clark, Tavistock Street, London, 1826, p 1131.
9. Fishwick Henry, *History of Garstang*, Chetham Society, part 2, 1878, pp 161–175.
10. Nightingale B, *Lancashire Nonconformity*, John Heywood, Deansgate, Manchester, 1890, vol 1, p 191.
11. *The Complete Works of that Eminent Minister of God's Word, Mr Isaac*

Ambrose, Gil, Martin and Jo. Wotherspoon, Advocate's Close, Luckenbooths, Edinburgh, 1761, passim.

12. Axon Ernest, *The Kings' Preachers in Lancashire, 1599–1845*, Transactions of the Lancashire and Cheshire Antiquarian Society, vol LVI, 1941–2, passim.
13. Abram W. Alexander, *The Rolls of Burgesses at the Guild Merchant of Preston 1397–1682*, The Record Society, 1884, p 95.
14. Fishwick Henry, op. cit., p 167.
15. *The Complete Works of that Eminent Minister of God's Word, Mr Isaac Ambrose*, op. cit.
16. Fishwick Henry, *History of Garstang*, op. cit. pp 167–8.
17. Calamy Edmund DD., *The Nonconformists Memorial*, W Harris, 70 St Paul's Churchyard, London, vol 2, 1775, p 93.
18. Nightingale B, *Centenary of the Lancashire Congregational Union 1806–1906*, op, cit., opposite p 69.

Chapter Two

1. Robinson W. Gordon, MA, BD, PhD *A History of the Lancashire Congregational Union 1806–1956*, Lancashire Congregational Union, 244 Deansgate, Manchester 3, p 163.
2. *Lancashire Congregational Calendar, 1867–71*, LRO Ref CUL/3/1.
3. Nightingale B, *Lancashire Nonconformity*, John Heywood, Deansgate, Manchester, 1890, vol 1, p 194.
4. *Preston Guardian*, 21 May 1927.
5. Nightingale B, *Lancashire Nonconformity*, op. cit., p 194.
6. Nightingale B, *Centenary of the Lancashire Congregational Union 1806–1906*, John Heywood Ltd, Manchester, pp 5–7, 12.
7. Robinson W. Gordon, *A History of the Lancashire Congregational Union 1806–1956*, op. cit., pp 20–1.
8. Ibid, p 163.
9. *Map accompanying lease of land on which to erect a school, 1756*, LRO Ref DDX 386/1.
10. *Churchwardens' Religious Census, 1755*, Garstang, Churchtown, Victorian County History, part 26c, p 299.
11. *Quarter Sessions, Lancaster*, 15 July 1707.
12. Heath Sylvia, *Preston Guardian*, Newspaper cutting, *c.* 1951.
13. Johnson Carolyn (Owner) *Correspondence* with Brenda Fox.
14. Allen Richard, *History of Methodism in Preston and its Vicinity*, Toulmin Printer, Preston, 1866, p 20.
15. Hewitson Anthony, *Our Country Churches and Chapels*, Chronicle Office, London, 1872, p 482.
16. Porteus W B., *Notes on the History of St Thomas' Church, Garstang*, 1970.
17. Bamber R N., *A History of Saints Mary and Michael, Bonds, Garstang*, Amblers Printers, Preston, 1994, p 14.

18. Hewitson Anthony, *Our Country Churches and Chapels*, op. cit., p 492.
19. Nightingale B, *Centenary of the Lancashire Congregational Union 1806–1906*, op. cit., p 84.
20. Nightingale B, *Lancashire Nonconformity*, op. cit., p 202.
21. Hewitson Anthony, *Our Country Churches and Chapels*, op. cit., p 483.
22. Cartmell Edward, *Notes* (CR).
23. Ibid.
24. Murgatroyd Thomas, *Invoice for Building Work*, 1867 (CR).
25. Stewart R J, *Renovation and Repair to the United Reformed Church, Garstang*, Project for HNC Civil Engineering, 1984.
26. Schedule: *Particulars and Valuation of the Township of Garstang*, the Property of F W Keppel Esq 1840, LRO Ref P 144/3.

Chapter Three

1. McLaughlin E., *Nonconformist Ancestors*, A McLaughlin Guide, 1995, p 2.
2. *Garstang Independent Chapel Register*, LRO Ref MF 1/71.
3. Edmondson James, *Will*, made 17 December 1792.
4. *Parish Registers of Chipping*, LRO Ref MF 2/ 44–53.
5. Nightingale B., *Lancashire Nonconformity*, John Heywood, Deansgate, Manchester, vol 1, 1890, p 195.
6. Ibid, p 227.
7. *Garstang Independent Chapel Register*, LRO Ref MF 1/71.
8. Ibid.
9. Hewitson Anthony, *Our Country Churches and Chapels*, Chronicle Office, London, 1872, p 467.
10. Ibid, p 475.
11. Bamber R. N., *Garstang & District Agricultural and Horticultural Society, A History*, Colin Cross, Printers, Garstang, 1988, p 9.
12. Russell Colin, *Lancastrian Chemist*, Open University Press, Milton Keynes, 1986.
13. Allen Richard, *History of Methodism in Preston and its Vicinity*, Toulmin Printer, Preston, 1866, p 20.
14. *Indenture for Purchase of Land from Keppel Estate*, 16 March 1867 (CR).
15. Armstrong William, *Will*, husbandman of Kirkland, made January 1807, proved November 1809.
16. Topham Robert, *Will*, yeoman of Barnacre, made July 1790, proved May 1792.

Chapter Four

1. Bell William, *Photo*, Preston Guardian, 21 May 1927.
2. Bell William, *Signature*, Church Register. LRO Ref MF 1/71.
3. Bell William, *Obituary*, Preston Guardian, 19 Nov 1870.

4. Ibid.
5. *IGI* Stirlingshire, Scotland.
6. *Elswick Congregational Chapel Records*, LRO Ref MF 1/70.
7. *Garstang Independent Chapel Register*, LRO Ref MF 1/71.
8. Hewitson Anthony, *Our Country Churches and Chapels*, John Heywood, Deansgate, Manchester. 1872, p 482.
9. Nightingale B., *Lancashire Nonconformity*, John Heywood, Deansgate, Manchester. 1890, vol 1, p 189.
10. Nightingale B., *History of the Old Independent Chapel, Tockholes*, John Heywood, Deansgate, Manchester, 1886, p 111.
11. Nightingale B., *Lancashire Nonconformity*, op. cit., p 196.
12. Ibid, p 196.
13. Ibid, p 203.
14. Hewitson Anthony, *Our Country Churches and Chapels*, op. cit., p 483.
15. *Preston Chronicle*, 29 August 1829.
16. Ibid, 15 August 1829.
17. Henderson W.O., *Industrial Britain under the Regency, 1814–1818*, Frank Cass, London, 1968, p 103, citing *Diary of Johann Georg Bodmer (1788–1864)*.
18. Russell Colin, *Lancastrian Chemist,* Open University Press, Milton Keynes, 1986, citing *appendix to the First Report of the Poor Law Commission, 1832–4*, p 924 A.
19. *Preston Chronicle*, 30 January, 1830.
20. Ibid, 18 December, 1830.
21. *Minutes of Preston District, Lancashire Congregational Union*, February 1832, LRO Ref CUPF/16.
22. Ibid, February 1833.
23. *An Act for the Abolition of the Slave Trade*, 25 March 1807.
24. *Preston Chronicle*, 4 December 1830.
25. Ibid, 18 December 1830.
26. *House of Lords Journal*, volume 63, 20 December, 1830.
27. *Correspondence* between Simon Gough, Parliamentary Archives Officer, and Brenda Fox.
28. *Minutes of Preston District, Lancashire Congregational Union*, February 1835, LRO Ref CUPE/16.
29. Nightingale B., *Lancashire Nonconformity*, op. cit., p 198.
30. *Schedule: Particulars and Valuation of the Township of Garstang*, the Property of F W Keppel Esq, 1840, LRO Ref P144/3.
31. *Sale Catalogue of the Lordship of Garstang, 1867*, LRO Ref DDX 1096/12.
32. Tucket Philip, *Plan of the Lordship of Garstang, 1867*, Norfolk Record Office Ref MF/RO 570/6, BRA 983/150.
33. Threlfall Henry, *Ledger*, LRO Ref DDX 1096/3.
34. *Garstang Corporation Record Book*, LRO Ref DDX 386/8.
35. *Garstang Union Records*, 1844–1849, LRO Ref PUY/1/2.

36. Bell William, *Obituary*, op. cit.
37. *Correspondence* between Edward Cartmell and Thomas Hamer, 1881/2 (CR).
38. *Minutes of Deacon's Meeting*, 24 September 1882 (CR).

Chapter Five

1. *Census, Garstang*, 1841.
2. *Schedule: Particulars and Valuation of the Township of Garstang*, the Property of F W Keppel Esq, 1840, LRO Ref P144/3.
3. Nightingale B., *Lancashire Nonconformity*, John Heywood, Deansgate, Manchester, 1890, vol 1, p 199.
4. *Church members* (CR).
5. Cartmell Edward, *Notes* (CR).
6. *Minutes of Preston District*, Lancashire Congregational Union, LRO Ref CUPF/16, February 1840.
7. *Quarter Sessions Petitions*, LRO Ref QSP 2698/19.
8. *Library Books* (CR).
9. *Seat Rents Book* (CR).
10. Cartmell Edward, *Notes* (CR).
11. Weston James, *Joseph Livesey: the Story of his Life 1794–1884*, S W Partridge & Co., Paternoster Row, 1884.
12. Winskill P T., *The Comprehensive History of the Rise and Progress of the Temperance Reformation*, Winskill, Bewsey Street, Warrington, 1881, p 80.
13. *Minutes of Preston District*, Lancashire Congregational Union, February 1835, LRO Ref CUPF/16.
14. *Church Members* (CR).
15. Nightingale B., *Lancashire Nonconformity*, op. cit., p 200.
16. *Minutes of the Preston District*, Lancashire Congregational Union, op. cit., February 1849.
17. Ibid, February 1850.
18. Murgatroyd Thomas, *Invoice*, 1867 (CR).
19. *Religious Census 1851,* LRO Ref MF 28/4.
20. Nightingale B., *Lancashire Nonconformity*, op. cit., p 202.
21. *Church Members* (CR).
22. Nightingale B., *Lancashire Nonconformity*, op. cit., p 200.
23. *Minutes of Preston District*, Lancashire Congregational Union, op. cit., February 1857.
24. Nightingale B., *Centenary of the Lancashire Congregational Union 1806–1906*, John Heywood Ltd., Manchester, p 188.
25. *Minutes of Preston District*, Lancashire Congregational Union, op. cit., February 1860.

Chapter Six

1. *Preston Guardian*, 3 May 1890.
2. Sharpe France R., County Archivist, *Lancashire Acts of Parliament 1415–1800*, Record Publications No 3, 1950.
3. *Preston Guardian*, 27 April 1867.
4. Ibid, 22 June 1867.
5. *Lancaster Guardian*, 26 November 1859.
6. *Indenture*, LRO Ref DDX 619/3/4.
7. *Conveyance of Freehold*, LRO Ref CUL 8/172.
8. *Preston Guardian*, 18 April 1868.
9. *Sale Catalogue*, LRO Ref DDX 1096/12.
10. *Preston Guardian*, 22 June 1867.
11. Ibid, 20 July 1867.
12. *Sale Document*, November 1919, LRO Ref DDX 131/1.
13. *Preston Guardian*, 18 April 1868.
14. *Pamphlet requesting Donations for Repair of the Chapel* (CR).
15. *Preston Guardian*, 18 April 1868.
16. Murgatroyd Thomas, *Invoice*, 1867 (CR).
17. Alston William, Glovers Court, Preston, *Invoice*, Xmas 1867 (CR).
18. Collinson Jonathan, Nateby Works, *Invoice*, 11 Feb 1868 (CR).
19. *Garstang Chapel Building Account*, 27 March 1869 (CR).
20. *Preston Guardian*, 18 April 1868.

Chapter Seven

1. *Minutes*, 11 July 1871 (CR).
2. Ibid, 8 August 1871 (CR).
3. Ibid, 21 January 1872 (CR).
4. Palgrave-Moore Patrick, *Understanding the History and Records of Nonconformity*, Elvery Dowers Publications, 1994, p 16.
5. *Marriage Register*, Forton Congregational Church, 15 June 1860.
6. *Chapel Accounts Book (1871–1890)*, 1 September 1871, pp 202–3 (CR).
7. *Marriage Register*, 6 September 1871 (CR).
8. *Census,* Scorton, 1841, 1851.
9. *Marriage Register*, 25 October 1871 (CR).
10. *Chapel Accounts Book (1871–1890)*, pp 1–33 (CR).
11. *Minutes*, 8 August 1871 (CR).
12. Ibid, 31 December 1875 (CR).
13. Ibid, 11 October 1872 (CR).
14. *Chapel Accounts Book (1871–1890)*, 24 August 1872, p 15 (CR).
15. Hewitson Anthony, *Our Country Churches and Chapels*, Chronicle Office, Fishergate, Preston, 1872, pp 467–484.

16. *Minutes*, 22 July 1872 (CR).
17. Ibid, 3 January 1873 (CR).
18. *Transactions of the Independent Chapel, Garstang*, pp 22–23a (CR).
19. *Minutes*, 16 May 1873 (CR).
20. Cartmell Edward, *Notebook* (CR).

Chapter Eight

1. *Minutes*, 11 March 1875 (CR).
2. Ibid, 2 August 1875 (CR).
3. *Preston Guardian*, 11 December 1875.
4. *Minutes*, 3 November 1875 (CR).
5. Cartmell Edward, *Notebook–Garstang Congregational Chapel Tea Meeting*, 1875 (CR).
6. *Preston Guardian*, 11 December 1875.
7. *Minutes*, February 1876 (CR).
8. Ibid, 5 April 1876 (CR).
9. *Transactions of the Independent Chapel, Garstang*, Manse Account, p 33c (CR).
10. Ibid, *Letter* re: Richard Helm of Leyland, May 1877, p 33b (CR).
11. Risque, Robson & Yates, solicitors, *Letter* to W H Cartmell, 26 May 1928 (CR).
12. *Minutes*, 1 September 1876.
13. *Census*, Garstang, 1881.
14. *List of Trustees*, Appointed 20 May 1898 (CR).
15. *Minutes*, 13 April 1877 (CR).
16. Ibid, 31 December 1916 (CR).
17. *Secretary's pre-war correspondence*, LRO Ref CUL/8/172.
18. *Minutes of Preston District*, Lancashire Congregational Union, 2 November 1864, LRO Ref CUPE/16.
19. *Minutes*, 2 January 1877 (CR).
20. *Lady Hewley's Trust*, LRO Ref CUL/9/109.
21. *Minutes*, 16 May 1879 (CR).
22. Ibid, 14 August 1879 (CR).
23. *Newspaper Cutting*, 10 June 1877, in Chapel Accounts Book 1871–1890 (CR).
24. *Sermon*, 1969, LRO Ref DDX 2743.
25. *The New World Library Encyclopaedia*, The Caxton Publishing Co Ltd, 1965.
26. *Preston Guardian*, 21 June 1879.
27. *Reports*, 1876, '77, '78, in Chapel Accounts Book 1871–1890 (CR).
28. Cartmell, Edward, *Notebook* (CR).
29. *Invoices*, 1895 (CR).
30. *Transactions of the Independent Chapel, Garstang*, p1 (CR).
31. *Minutes*, 29 November 1884 (CR).

Chapter Nine

1. *Minutes*, 4 April 1880 (CR).
2. Cockram, Joseph, *Photograph,* in possession of his descendants.
3. *Minutes*, 20 July 1880 (CR).
4. Ibid, 29 September 1880.
5. Ibid, 16 November 1880.
6. *Chapel Account Book 1871–1890*, 8 March 1881, 4 July 1881 (CR).
7. Clark James, *Letters* to Edward Cartmell, 1881 (CR).
8. *Minutes*, June 1882 (CR).
9. Ibid, 22 May 1881.
10. Cockram Revd Joseph, *Letter* to Edward Cartmell, 1 June 1881 (CR).
11. Mansergh Robert, *Letter* to Edward Cartmell, 7 July 1881 (CR).
12. Cartmell Robert, *Letter*, 2 June 1881 (CR).
13. *Minutes,* 1 June 1881 (CR).
14. Cockram Revd Joseph, *Letter* to Edward Cartmell, 2 October 1881 (CR).
15. *Minutes*, 15 November 1993 (CR).
16. Ibid, 2 November 1881 (CR).
17. *Band of Hope Pledge Card* (CR).
18. *Band of Hope Notebook* (CR).
19. *Minutes,* 12 July 1882 (CR).
20. Ibid, 10 October 1883.
21. Ibid, 24 September 1882.
22. Ibid, 27 December 1882.
23. Ibid, 4 February 1883.
24. *Minutes Forton Congregational Church*, 31 January 1883.
25. *Minutes Garstang Congregational Church*, 29 November 1884.
26. *Photograph*, in possession of Joseph Cockram's descendants.
27. *Extract from Mid-Westmoreland Herald*, 27 October 1900, plus appeal from office holders of the Lancashire Congregational Union.

Chapter Ten

1. *Census,* Scorton, 1851.
2. *Preston Chronicle & Lancashire Advertiser*, 10 June 1848.
3. *Chapel Accounts Book 1871–1890*, 1872–1877 (CR).
4. *Census*, Barnacre-with-Bonds, 1881.
5. Hall Liliane Bell (née Hamer), *Letter* to Mr Herbert Cartmell, 27 April 1953 (CR).
6. Le Mare Peter H, *The Le Mare Family from about 1700*, www.Lemare.org, pp 33–34.
7. *Minutes*, 30 December 1885 (CR).
8. *List of Church Members*, 4 March 1883 (CR).
9. *Sunday School Register*, 1882 (CR).

10. *List of Church Members*, December 1883 (CR).
11. *Register of Band of Hope and Temperance Society Members* (CR).
12. *Minutes*, September 1886 (CR).
13. *Preston Guardian*, 2 July, 1887.
14. *Lancaster Guardian*, 2 July, 1887.
15. *Minutes,* 21 May 1884.
16. Ibid, 23 October 1885.
17. Ibid, 2 November 1887.
18. Thomas, J. J., *Invoices*, to Independent Chapel (CR).
19. *Chapel Accounts Book 1871–1890*, pp 182–188 (CR).
20. *Minutes*, 15 March 1881 (CR).
21. Ibid, 16 November 1880.
22. Ibid, 15 March 1881.
23. Ibid, 19 December 1883.
24. Ibid, 14 August 1883.
25. *Newspaper Cutting 1883*, Accounts Book, 1871–1890, p 0 (CR).
26. *Chapel Accounts Book 1871–1890*, p 98 (CR).
27. *Burial Register*, 12 August 1888 (CR).
28. Hall, Liliane Bell (née Hamer), *Letter*, op.cit., 1953 (CR).
29. Knight, Elsie, *A Life and History of Fleetwood Congregational Church and United Reformed Church*, 1998, Printed Privately.

Chapter Eleven

1. *Minutes*, 4 November 1888 (CR).
2. *Minutes of Preston District*, Lancashire Congregational Union (LCU), 1890, LRO Ref CUP f/28.
3. *Minutes*, 14 November 1888 (CR).
4. *Minutes of Preston District* (LCU), op. cit., 1890.
5. *Preston Guardian,* 3 May 1890.
6. *Minutes of Preston District* (LCU), op. cit., 1891.
7. Nightingale B., *Lancashire Nonconformity*, John Heywood, Deansgate, Manchester, 1890, vol 1, pp 201–2.
8. *Minutes*, 20 September 1889 (CR).
9. *Subscription Book*, 1889/90 (CR).
10. *Lancaster Division Electors Guide*, February 1889.
11. *Minutes*, 20 September 1889 (CR).
12. *Chapel Accounts Book 1871–1890*, p 123 (CR).
13. *Preston Guardian*, 5 April 1890.
14. Ibid, 3 May 1890.
15. *Minutes Preston District* (LCU), op. cit., 1891.
16. *Minutes*, 8 April 1891 (CR).
17. *Chapel Accounts Book 1871–1890*, p 125 (CR).

18. *Lancaster Guardian*, 3 May 1890.
19. *Preston Guardian*, 10 May 1890.
20. *Minutes*, 8 April 1891 (CR).
21. Ibid, 1 July 1891 (CR).

Chapter Twelve

1. *Minutes*, 22 December 1891 (CR).
2. *Preston Guardian*, 21 May 1927.
3. Vicar and Churchwardens of Over Wyresdale Church, *Receipt*, 29 June 1893 (CR).
4. *Minutes*, 4 July 1893 (CR).
5. Helme John, *Invoice*, Midsummer 1893 (CR).
6. Ainscough H, *Description of Organ*, 31 August 1893 (CR).
7. *Minutes*, 16 August 1893 (CR).
8. *Poster*, 1893 (CR).
9. *Minutes*, 15 November 1893 (CR).
10. Ibid, 6 November 1894.
11. Ibid, 1 May 1895.
12. Heathcote R, *Invoice*, 27 May 1895 (CR).
13. *Minutes*, 12 June 1895 (CR).
14. *Poster*, 1895 (CR).
15. Dr Brooke Westcott, *photograph*, in possession of his great-grandson, Brooke Westcott.
16. *Lancaster Guardian*, 2 December 1890.
17. Ibid, 27 December 1890.
18. Ibid, 29 December 1894.
19. *Preston Guardian*, 29 December 1894.
20. *Lancaster Guardian*, 23 November 1894.
21. *Minutes*, 5 July 1896 (CR).
22. Ibid, 28 April 1897 (CR).
23. Ibid, 31 March 1897 (CR).
24. Ibid, 16 June 1897 (CR).
25. Ibid, 1 June 1897 (CR).
26. *Preston Guardian*, 5 June 1897.
27. Ibid, 12 June 1897.
28. *Burke's Peerage and Baronetage*, 106th edition, volume 1, p 48.
29. *The Graphic* (London), 26 June 1897.
30. *The Morning Post*, 21 June 1897.
31. *The Hampshire Advertiser*, 23 June 1893.
32. *Minutes*, 1 June 1897 (CR).
33. *Preston Guardian*, 26 June 1897.
34. *Lancaster Guardian*, 26 June 1897.

35. Ibid, 26 June 1897.
36. *Minutes*, 6 July 1898 (CR).
37. Ibid, 29 June 1898 (CR).
38. *Preston Guardian*, 13 November 1897.
39. *Preston Guardian*, 13 November 1897.
40. *Bazaar Balance Sheet*, November 1897 (CR).
41. *Minutes*, 5 January 1898 (CR).

Chapter Thirteen

1. Cartmell *Marriage Records*, LRO Ref DDX/1223/14.
2. *Census*, Barnacre-with- Bonds, 1841–1901.
3. Cartmell John, *Obituary*, Preston Guardian, Saturday, 5 April 1902.
4. Kelly's *Directory of Lancashire*, 1905.
5. *Monumental Inscription*, Garstang URC.
6. Cartmell John, *Obituary*, op. cit.
7. *Sunday School Records* (CR).
8. *Seat Rents Book* (CR).
9. Cartmell *Marriage Records*, LRO Ref DDX/1223/13.
10. *Preston Guardian*, Saturday 30 March, 1907.
11. Cartmell Edward (Ted), *Letter*, to Brenda Fox.
12. Cartmell Edward, *Obituary*, Preston Guardian, Saturday 30 March, 1907.
13. Cartmell Edward, *Obituary*, Lancashire Daily Post, Tuesday 2 April, 1907.
14. *Cartmell Marriage Records*, LRO Ref DDX/1223/14.
15. *Census*, Garstang, 1881–1901.
16. Cartmell John, *Obituary*, Preston Guardian, Saturday 9 April, 1927.
17. *Church Marriage Records*, 1902.
18. *Oral evidence* given by Isaac Storey, nephew of Richard (Dick) Storey, to Paul Smith.
19. Cartmell *Marriage Records*, LRO Ref DDX/1223/14.
20. *Monumental Inscription*, Garstang URC.
21. *Minutes*, 15 November 1893 (CR).
22. Cartmell Robert, *Obituary*, Preston Guardian, Saturday 23 October, 1897.
23. Cartmell *Marriage Records*, LRO Ref DDX/1223/14.
24. *Census*, Barton, 1881.
25. *Monumental Inscription*, Garstang URC.
26. *Census*, Garstang, 1891.
27. *Bazaar Booklet*, 1897 (CR).
28. *Church Records*, passim.
29. Cartmell Moses, *Obituary*, Preston Guardian, Saturday 27 April, 1917.
30. Cartmell Edward (Ted), *Letter*, to Brenda Fox.
31. Cartmell W. Harold, *Obituary*, Preston Guardian, 26 January, 1957.
32. *Church Records*, passim.

33. *Church Visitors' Reports*, 15 January, 1934, LRO Ref CUL 6/60.
34. Ibid, 16 November, 1934.
35. Ibid, 12 December, 1946.
36. *Preston Guardian*, 21 May 1927.
37. Cartmell Edward (Ted), *Letter*, to Brenda Fox.
38. Ibid.
39. Cartmell Herbert, *Obituary*, Preston Guardian, 30 November 1962.
40. *Minutes*, 27 January 1964 (CR).
41. *Church Records*, passim.
42. Cartmell Kath, *Obituary*, Garstang Courier, 16 August 1985.
43. Robinson W Gordon, *A History of the Lancashire Congregational Union 1806–1956*, LCU, 244 Deansgate, Manchester 3, p 180.
44. *Minutes*, 20 April 1931 (CR).
45. *Oral evidence* given by Eileen Green, daughter-in-law of Dorothy (née Cartmell).
46. *Minutes*, 20 April 1931 (CR).
47. Cartmell Edward (Ted), *Letter*, to Brenda Fox.
48. Cartmell Edward (Ted), *Legacy*, Plaque in Garstang URC Church Hall.
49. Cartmell Edward (Ted), *Letter*, to Brenda Fox.
50. *Details on Stained Glass Window*, Garstang URC.
51. Cartmell Edward (Ted), *Letter*, to Brenda Fox.

Chapter Fourteen

1. Sharpe France R, County Archivist, *Lancashire Acts of Parliament 1415–1800*, Record Publication Number 3, 1950.
2. *Anecdotes of the Duchess of Gloucester,* The Gentleman's and London Magazine: or Monthly Chronology, 1784, pp 317–319.
3. *Lancaster Guardian*, 26 November 1859, p 5.
4. Farrer William and Brownbill J (Editors), *The Victoria History of the Counties of England*, Amounderness Hundred, Constable and Co Ltd, London, 1912, p 311.
5. Burke Bernard Sir LLD, *Dictionary of the Peerage and Baronetage of the British Empire*, Harrison, 59 Pall Mall, London, 1864, 26th edition, pp 19, 934, 935.
6. *Land Tax Assessment*, Garstang, 1785, LRO Ref QDL/A/26.
7. *Declaration of Release*, 2 February 1859, LRO Ref DDX 619/2.
8. *Declaration of Release*, 9 August 1875, LRO Ref DDX 619/3.
9. *Declaration of Release*, 27 October 1875, LRO Ref DDX 619/4.
10. *Preston Guardian*, 8 November 1919.
11. *Garstang Show Catalogue*, 1939.
12. *Bishop Frederick Keppel*, details of his life, Exeter Cathedral Archives.
13. *Census*, Barnacre with Bonds, 1891.

14. *Historical Notes on the Doggett Family*, LRO Ref DDX 264/41–48.
15. *Census*, Barnacre with Bonds, 1901.
16. Nightingale B., *Centenary of the Lancashire Congregational Union 1806 – 1956*, John Heywood Ltd., Deansgate, Manchester, opp. p 161.
17. Ibid, opposite p 156.
18. *Lancashire Congregational Year Book*, 1914. LRO Ref CUL/3/36 p64.
19. Nightingale B., op. cit., p 162.
20. Robinson W Gordon, *A History of the Lancashire Congregational Union 1806–1956*, Lancashire Congregational Union, 244 Deansgate, Manchester 3, 1955, pp 179, 180.
21. *Preston Guardian*, 6 and 13 May, 1916.
22. *Preston Guardian*, 2 July, 1904.
23. *Lancashire Congregational Year Book*, 1914, op. cit.
24. *Preston Guardian*, 13 November 1897, p7.
25. *Census*, Staynall, 1881.
26. *Census*, Garstang, 1891.
27. *Sunday School and Band of Hope Registers*, Congregational Chapel, Garstang (CR).
28. Cartmell Edward (Ted), *Letter* to Brenda Fox.
29. *Advertisement,* Church Bazaar Book, 1897 (CR).
30. *Census,* Garstang, 1881.
31. *Marriages, Cartmell Records,* LRO Ref DDX 1223/14.
32. *Baptism* Sidney H C Cartmell, 7 October 1883 (CR).
33. *Burial Records* (CR).
34. *Band of Hope and Temperance Records,* 1900 (CR).
35. *Church Minutes*, 16 April, 1907 (CR).
36. *Church Minutes*, 17 July, 1901 (CR).
37. *WW1 Army Records*, WO/363 (Burnt Documents), National Archives, Kew.
38. Edmunds J E Brigadier, *Official History of the Great War*, HMSO.
39. *WWI Army Records*, WO/363 op. cit.
40. *Correspondence from War Graves' Commission* (CR).
41. *Ordnance Survey Map*, 6 inch, First edition, 1841.
42. Keppel Frederick Walpole, *Wages Book*, LRO Ref DDX 1096/4.
43. Le Mare Peter H., *The Le Mare Family from about 1700*, www.Lemare.org.

• INDEX •